Healthy Habits

for

Spiritual Growth

Argeina _____

signature

Prov 31:30
Phil 1:6

Discovery House PUBLISHERS

BOX 3566 · GRAND RAPIDS, MI 49501

*PUBLISHING BOOKS THAT FEED
THE SOUL WITH THE WORD OF GOD.*

Healthy Habits
FOR
Spiritual Growth

52 Principles for Personal Change

Luis Palau

Healthy Habits for Spiritual Growth:
52 Principles for Personal Change
Copyright © 1994 Luis Palau

Discovery House Publishers is affiliated with Radio Bible Class, Grand Rapids, Michigan 49501

Discovery House books are distributed to the trade by Thomas Nelson Publishers, Nashville, Tennessee 37214

Unless otherwise indicated, Scripture is taken from the HOLY BIBLE, NEW INTERNATIONAL VERSION. Copyright © 1973, 1978, 1984 International Bible Society. Used by permission of Zondervan Bible Publishers.

Library of Congress Cataloging-in-Publication Data

Palau, Luis, 1934—
    Healthy habits for spiritual growth : 52 principles for personal change / Luis Palau.
    p. cm.
    ISBN 0-929239-87-3

    1. Spiritual formation. 2. Bible. N.T. Epistles of Paul—Criticism, interpretation, etc. 3. Devotional calendars. I. Title.
BV4501.2.P2664   1994
248.4—dc20   94-8633
                                                                              CIP

Printed in the United States of America

96 97 98 99 / CHG / 10 9 8 7 6 5 4 3

Dedication

To the glory of God for the building up of His family.
Day by day, as you prayerfully read, digest, and
practice the healthy habits of God's Word explained
in this book, you will bring honor to God. So I
dedicate this book to our Father in heaven.

And I also dedicate *Healthy Habits for Spiritual Growth* to
my colleague and young friend, David Sanford.
David, you have made my thoughts clear, readable,
engaging, appealing, vibrant, and useful. The Lord richly
reward you!

Contents

Introduction

Thank God His grace isn't "fair."

A couple of years ago, one of my nephews (I'll call him Kenneth) was near death. Once the picture of health, he now had AIDS. During a family reunion in the hills of northern California, Kenneth and I broke away for a short walk. He was a hollow shell, laboring for breath.

"Kenneth, you know you're going to die any day," I said. "Do you have eternal life? Your parents agonize. I must know."

"Luis, I know God has forgiven me and I'm going to heaven."

For several years, since his early teens, Kenneth had practiced homosexuality. More than that, in rebellion against God and his parents, he flaunted his lifestyle.

"Kenneth, how can you say that?" I replied. "You rebelled against God, you made fun of the Bible, you hurt your family terribly. And now you say you've got eternal life, just like that?"

"Luis, when the doctor said I had AIDS, I realized what a fool I'd been."

"We know that," I said bluntly but deliberately, because Kenneth knew full well what Romans 1 teaches. "But did you really repent?"

"I did repent, and I know God has had mercy on me. But my dad won't believe me."

"With good reason," I said. "You've rebelled in his face all your life. You've broken his heart."

Kenneth looked me straight in the eye. "I know the Lord has forgiven me."

"Did you open your heart to Jesus?"

"Yes, Luis! Yes!"

As we put our arms around each other and prayed and talked some more, I became convinced that Jesus had forgiven all of Kenneth's rebellion and washed away his sin. Several short months later, he went to be with the Lord, at age twenty-five.

My nephew, like the repentant thief on the cross, certainly didn't deserve God's grace. I didn't either. None of us does. That's why grace is grace—unmerited favor.

I've sometimes found it hard to be kind and patient with someone who has openly, purposefully, and recklessly broken a basic command of God and then is suffering the consequences. Until Kenneth put a human face on AIDS and homosexual sin, it was with trepidation—never too loud—that I'd say, "God loves homosexuals."

My nephew has made me more tender, and more bold, in discussing God's forgiveness with anyone who has committed blatant sin, whatever it may be, if that person truly repents.

Still, it doesn't come easy. In churches across America, I enter the danger zone when I say with conviction, "God loves homosexuals. Amen?"

There aren't many amens. Stone faces shout by their silence, "That isn't fair!"

Neither is grace.

God is like the owner of the vineyard who paid the same wage to workers who labored only one hour as he did to those who labored all day (Matthew 20:1–16). "You have made them equal to us who have borne the burden of the work and the heat of the day," they complained. Wouldn't you?

Replied the landowner, "Don't I have the right to do what I want with my own money? Or are you envious because I am generous?"

God's grace is generosity *extraordinaria*, love without limits. In those agonizing moments of Grace lifted up from the earth, our sins—all of them—were washed away by Jesus' blood so God could redeem us, adopt us, make us His children.

Unlike my nephew and the thief on the cross, however, most of us find ourselves pilgrims here on this earth. Unless Jesus comes back soon, you and I have years before us to work out what it means to be God's child.

Will they be years cultivating healthy habits, or years sowing destructive patterns? Years of growing dependence upon and obedience to the Lord, or years of frustration and fruitlessness?

Maybe you've recently trusted Jesus Christ for salvation. Perhaps you came to Christ through the witness of a friend, at an evangelistic crusade, by reading an evangelistic book, or via a gospel program on television or radio. Whatever the case, now you want to know, *What difference does it make that I'm a Christian?*

Or maybe you've been a Christian for some time. Perhaps you've seen a few changes in your life, but you haven't experienced the tremendous reality that can be yours thanks to the Lord.

If you practice the principles outlined in this book, I'm convinced you'll gain a whole new appreciation for your relationship with God. And, before you turn the last page, you'll see the powerful difference He can make in your life. Even better, others will see God at work in and through you!

I believe God wants to bless your life and use you to be a blessing to many others. Here's my prayer: "By his power, [may God] fulfill every good purpose of yours and every act prompted by your faith. We pray this so that the name of our Lord Jesus may be glorified in you, and you in him" (2 Thessalonians 1:11–12).

How to Read This Book

Whatever you do, don't read this book and then simply lay it aside. Put it to work!

After a quick initial reading (skimming over the application sections at the end of each chapter), start over and read this book again more slowly. This time have a Bible, notebook, and pen handy. Make notes about applying each habit. Underline or highlight any statements or sections in the book that seem especially significant to you.

Review this book again in a few weeks. Especially note the statements and sections you highlighted or underlined the second time through. Use a different colored pen to make additional notes. Ask God to help you cultivate each of the habits presented in this book.

Then, if *Healthy Habits for Spiritual Growth* is a help to you, why not recommend it to a friend?

Finally, write to me, please! It would be great to hear how the Lord is using the principles in this book to change your life. My address is P.O. Box 1173, Portland, Oregon 97207. I look forward to corresponding with you.

Are you ready, then? Ready for a lifelong adventure? Ready to begin cultivating healthy habits from which you'll reap rewards for all eternity? Let's begin!

PART ONE

Enjoying Fellowship as God's Child

As God's children, you and I have the incredible privilege both of talking to God and listening to what He has to say to us!

■ *Habit*

Taking Time
to Pray

What is the one thing that most often keeps Christians from experiencing God's making a dramatic difference in their lives? Is it carelessness? Lack of good Christian fellowship? Temptation?

May I suggest *prayerlessness*?

How often do you and I receive answers to prayer? Many Christians have no idea what it means to be a child of God who can talk with the Lord about a real need, let alone to receive a specific, valid, and recognizable answer to their prayers.

I could tell you Bible promises on prayer, plus some of my own experiences and those of friends, but I can't do your praying for you. You can read all the manuals on prayer and listen to other people pray, but until you begin to pray yourself you will never understand prayer. It's like riding a bicycle or swimming: You learn by doing.

Martin Luther said, "Just as the business of the tailor is to make clothing, and that of the shoemaker to mend shoes, so the business of the Christian is to pray."

The secret of Luther's revolutionary life was his commitment to spend time alone with God every day.

"Consider the lives of the most outstanding and shining servants of God," J.C. Ryle challenges us, "whether they be in the Bible or out of the Bible. In all of them you will find that they were men of prayer. Depend on prayer; prayer is powerful."

I encourage you to take time every day to talk with God. Don't just give Him thirty seconds while you're rushing around in the morning: "O Lord, bless this day, especially since it is Monday. . . ." What kind of prayer is that?

It is essential to set aside a specific time each day for personal prayer. Strive for order and faithfulness, but avoid legalism. On certain occasions you may need to select a different time during the day to pray. Nothing is wrong with that. But strive for consistency.

I have found the early hours of the day are the best to pray. So have such men of God as Martin Luther in Germany, John Wesley in England, Hudson Taylor in China, and many others. Evangelist D.L. Moody echoed their sentiments when he said, "We ought to see the face of God every morning before we see the face of man. If you have so much business to attend to that you have no time to pray, depend upon it that you have more business on hand than God ever intended." Make room in your schedule to begin each day alone with God in prayer.

On the other hand, prayer is something that should take place during the entire day. The Bible says, "Pray continually" (1 Thessalonians 5:17). At any moment, whatever the occasion, we are free to speak with our Father. Albert J. Wollen says every Christian can enjoy "constant, conscious communion with God." We enjoy this communion with the living God, who lives within us, through prayer.

"If Jesus prayed, what about you? What about you?" asks the hymn writer. It's always surprising to see how much time Jesus dedicated to prayer. He never considered Himself too busy to pray. As the obligations increased and as He faced big decisions, He went away alone to pray. How about you?

TO PONDER

• Are you a child of God? If so, when do you pray to your heavenly Father? How would you describe your prayers?

• If you're not sure whether you're a child of God yet, I encourage you to read my booklet *What Is a Real Christian?* (Multnomah). Write to me to ask for your free copy.

TO PURSUE

• Take a minute right now to tell God, "I'd like to enjoy a rich time of fellowship with you—a time so rich, I'll want to spend even more time each day alone with you, praying."

• Set aside fifteen minutes tomorrow when you can be alone with the Lord in prayer. Guard that commitment. Then, tomorrow, show up several minutes early for your appointment with the King of kings!

Praying in God's Will

What is your favorite Bible promise? Is it a promise for strength? Courage? Security?

Allow me to share one of my favorite Scripture promises with you.

"This is the confidence we have in approaching God: that if we ask anything according to his will, he hears us. And if we know that he hears us —whatever we ask—we know that we have what we asked of him" (1 John 5:14–15).

Look at that! God has gone on record as saying that whatever we ask for according to His will, He will give it to us!

"There's only one problem, Luis," you say. "I don't know God's will. What good is this promise if I can only guess at His will?"

Fortunately, God has revealed much of His will in the Bible. By becoming better acquainted with God's Word, you will learn many things about His will for your life. His will is not hidden; it is revealed and written! Instead of speculating about God's sovereign will for tomorrow, we should focus on obeying His revealed will *today*. First John 5:14–15 promises that God will give us whatever we ask so we may do His will. This includes God's wisdom (James 1:5) and His strength (Isaiah 40:29–31).

If you are not sure a prayer request is according to God's will, ask Him about it; He can tell you. Don't worry about making mistakes when you pray. Do you think the sovereignty of God will be shattered because one of His children makes a mistake while praying? Isn't it a bigger mistake not to pray at all?

If the answer to your request is "no," the Lord will soon communicate that answer by the internal witness of the Holy Spirit. If you walk with God and have a consistent prayer life, then a sensitivity develops between you and your heavenly Father.

If God gently says "no" to a request you make, then He has something even better in store for you. Jesus says, "If you, then, though you are evil, know how to give good gifts to your children, how much more will your Father in heaven give good gifts to those who ask him!" (Matthew 7:11). If we ask for a worthless stone, He says "no" and gives us nourishing bread instead. God always gives us what is good.

We begin to experience the enthusiasm, joy, and excitement of the Christian life only as we claim God's promises through prayer.

Here are several promises that have been especially meaningful to me. I encourage you to make them a part of your life.

• "Delight yourself in the Lord and he will give you the desires of your heart" (Psalm 37:4).

• "The Lord will keep you from all harm—he will watch over your life; the Lord will watch over your coming and going both now and forevermore" (Psalm 121:7–8).

• "The name of the Lord is a strong tower; the righteous run to it and are safe" (Proverbs 18:10).

• "If you remain in me and my words remain in you, ask whatever you wish, and it will be given you" (John 15:7).

TO PONDER

• As a child of God, what is God's will for *you*? How do you know? How committed are you to obeying it?

TO PURSUE

• What is your favorite Bible promise? Take a minute to review it, then personalize it and turn it into a prayer to your heavenly Father.

Prayer That God Answers

God used D.L. Moody, the great nineteenth-century evangelist, to help bring two continents to repentance. It is estimated he traveled more than one million miles and preached the life-changing gospel of Jesus Christ to more than one hundred million people!

What characteristics made Moody stand out as God's man to reach the masses in Europe and North America? He was a man of faith. He was a man of purity. And he was a man of prayer. Moody asked God to move the mountains of unbelief in the souls of men and women, youth and children—and God answered!

Moody had this to say about prayer: "Some men's prayers need to be cut short at both ends and set on fire in the middle."

Are your prayers on fire? Are they prayers that reach the ear of God? Are they prayers that move the hearts of people?

Let me briefly describe the kind of prayer God delights to answer. If you take these principles to heart, watch for God to anoint your prayers with fire!

First, we must *believe*. Do you believe God is able and willing to answer your prayers? "I'm sure He is able," you say, "but I'm not so sure He is willing." Hebrews 11:6 says, "Without faith it is impossible to please God, because anyone who comes to him must believe that he exists and that he rewards those who earnestly seek him."

Prayerlessness is a problem, but an even more serious problem is unbelief. Many Christians don't believe God will actually grant their petitions. No wonder their prayers lack fire! The Bible clearly teaches that God answers prayer offered to Him in faith.

Second, we must *ask*. "You do not have, because you do not ask God" (James 4:2). Do you remember the story of the blind man in Mark 10? He was so excited about meeting Jesus. When they met, Jesus asked him, "What do you want me to do for you?" Jesus wanted to be asked! God wants to pour out His blessings if we will only ask.

The blind man came right to the point: "Rabbi, I want to see." He didn't beat around the bush, as we often do. We try to twist God's arm with our long, detailed petitions and explanations. What we need to do is cut off the flowery words and get to the point. That sets our prayers aflame.

Third, we must *confess sin*. The psalmist wrote, "If I had cherished sin in my heart, the Lord would not have listened" (Psalm 66:18). Sin douses the flames of prayer. Unconfessed sin extinguishes more prayers than we imagine.

King Saul anguished when he realized, toward the end of his life, that God no longer was answering his prayers (1 Samuel 28:6). He had let unconfessed sin build a wall between himself and God. Is anything standing between you and God? If so, confess your sins and experience the renewal of God in your life again.

Moody preceded each of his evangelistic crusades by urging God's people to pray. The fires of revival that swept various cities were not lit by Moody alone. They were ignited by the prayers of ordinary Christians who believed God, confessed their sins, and then offered prayers God delighted to answer.

TO PONDER

• As a child of God, do you find it easy or difficult to believe He hears and delights to answer your prayers? Why do you think you feel that way?

TO PURSUE

• Have you ever had any answers to prayer? What did you ask God and how did He answer? Take a minute or two to make a quick list of all the specific answers to prayer you can remember.

Praying with Expectancy and Thankfulness

You may be wondering if I will talk about any other healthy habits besides those related to prayer. I will! But I feel an urgency to impress you with the importance and joy of practicing consistent, effective, daily prayer.

Someone once remarked, "If I wished to humble anyone, I would question him about his prayers. I know nothing to compare with this topic for its sorrowful self-confessions."

The last thing I want to do is make someone feel guilty about not praying. Guilt is Satan's bitter substitute for action in the Christian life. Instead, God wants you to experience joy in your daily Christian walk. That is why Scripture encourages us to pray.

The Bible says, "Devote yourselves to prayer, being watchful and thankful" (Colossians 4:2). We should offer our requests with expectancy and thankfulness. We miss the joy of seeing prayer answered if we don't consciously watch for signs of God's intervention.

I encourage you to start a prayer notebook as a means of watching for God's answers to your prayers. Keeping a prayer notebook always motivates me to pray more frequently and specifically, and it helps me to sense the reality that I'm one of God's children.

First I write my requests in a notebook, along with the date I start making the request. If there is a deadline for a particular answer, I record that as well. Then in the other column I note when the Lord answers my prayers and what His answers are. It is exciting to see how God works!

My prayer notebook is a monument of the constant faithfulness of my heavenly Father. When I encounter difficult circumstances, I can reflect on God's faithfulness by reviewing how He has worked in my life in the past. Without a note-book I would soon forget many of God's marvelous answers to my prayers.

To start your own notebook, complete the exercise in prayer out-lined below. Then rejoice as you experience God's personal dealings in your life!

EXERCISE IN PRAYER

1. Think of one area in your life where you really need an answer to prayer.
2. Write it down and date it. Develop a prayer notebook.
3. Study the following passages on prayer in your Bible: Matthew 7:7–11; 18:19–20; Mark 10:46–52; John 16:24; Romans 8:26–27; Ephesians 6:10–20; James 5:16–18.
4. Simply and specifically tell the Lord your request.
5. Thank the Lord that He is going to answer your prayer (Philippi-ans 4:6).
6. Record the answer when it comes, and praise God for it (Coloss-ians 4:2).
7. Repeat!

How is your prayer life? You don't need to give a sorrowful con-fession. Instead, offer your requests with expectancy and thankful-ness. Use a prayer notebook to help you. Then share your blessings with other people. Be a living testimony that God still answers prayer!

TO PONDER

• Imagine the phone rings and someone conducting a national opinion poll asks, "Do you believe God still answers prayer today? If so, do you believe that (a) somewhat? (b) sincerely? or (c) strongly?" What would you say?

TO PURSUE

• If you don't already have a notebook, buy one the next time you go out. Then follow the instructions listed above to start your own prayer notebook. And don't forget to thank God for His answers!

Talking with God

"Prayer is friendship with God," Dr. James M. Houston once said. I think he made an important observation, for prayer is simply two friends talking together.

Prayer is a conversation between God and us, His children. It isn't a one-sided, one-track monologue of petitions, but a well-rounded dialogue. God speaks to us through His Word and the inner witness of the Holy Spirit. We respond to God with adoration, confession, petition, intercession, and thanksgiving. Without these five elements our prayers become lopsided and disproportional. Let's briefly consider these five aspects of prayer.

The first element of true prayer is *adoration*. As we enter God's presence in prayer, we begin by expressing our worship and reverence for Him. The Talmud gives this dictum: "Man should always first utter praises, and then pray." We find the praises of our Lord from past generations recorded throughout the pages of Scripture.

Confession follows our praise. When Isaiah saw the Lord in His glory, he cried, "Woe to me! I am ruined! For I am a man of unclean lips" (Isaiah 6:5). We cannot praise the God of holiness without developing a deep sense of our own uncleanness. The Bible also teaches us that God graciously forgives us when we confess our sins (1 John 1:9).

Only after adoration and confession do we offer our *petitions* to the Father. True prayer consists of the petitions of one who acknowledges his utter need, and the provisions of One who demonstrates His utter goodness.

Jesus gives us this promise: "Until now you have not asked for anything in my name. Ask and you will receive, and your joy will be complete" (John 16:24). He encourages us to ask the Father for what we need.

As we pray we should also include *intercession* for other people. What a ministry we can have at the throne of grace on behalf of others!

The prophet Samuel told the people of Israel, "Far be it from me that I should sin against the Lord by failing to pray for you" (1 Samuel 12:23). Intercession for others is an important spiritual responsibility we must not neglect as Christians.

Thanksgiving should naturally fill the remainder of our conversation with God. Listen to these exhortations from the apostle Paul: "Be joyful always; pray continually; give thanks in all circumstances, for this is God's will for you in Christ Jesus" (1 Thessalonians 5:16–18). We experience God's joy when we talk with Him in prayer and thank Him for His answers.

The great evangelist Charles Finney noted, "When God wants to bless His people, He first moves them to pray." He moves them to converse back and forth in a well-rounded dialogue.

Has God moved you to pray? Let's stop and talk with Him right now.

TO PONDER

• What is on your heart? About what do you want to talk with God? Do you feel moved to adore Him? Do you have something to confess? Do you have a specific petition?

TO PURSUE

• Take time, right now, to pray to your heavenly Father. Be sure to record any new petitions or matters of intercession in your prayer notebook.

Communion with God

Some years ago a doctor asked an elderly Christian woman in England, "If I asked God for five pounds, would I get it?"

The old woman answered with a question. "If you were introduced to the Prince of Wales, would you ask him for money at once?"

"No, not till I knew him better," replied the doctor.

"Well," remarked the woman, "you will need to know God a great deal better before you can expect Him to answer your prayer."

Someone commented on this incident by observing, "Many people presume to ask God for things upon mere acquaintance with Him." Isn't that often the case?

Prayer, as we said before, is simply two friends talking together. The Bible is God's side of the conversation. When I read the Scriptures, I soon find myself whispering a petition. When I pray, God's Word comes to mind. When I listen to His Word, my soul bows in adoration.

Bible expositor W. Graham Scroggie wrote, "In the Bible God speaks to us, and in prayer we speak to God." The Bible and prayer are intertwined strands forming the intimate cord of communion between God and ourselves.

Read the great prayers of Moses, Nehemiah, Ezra, and Daniel. In their petitions they spoke God's words back to Him. This is the prayer language God delights to answer. As you pray, let Him bring Scriptures to mind. Pray them back to God as they apply to you.

Before you spend time reading and studying the Bible each day, pray that God will make your heart sensitive to His Word. Martin Luther said, "Having prayed well is having studied well." We cannot have one without the other.

George Müller fellowshiped with God as few men in history have ever done. Through him, God cared for thousands of orphans. Despite his tremendous financial responsibilities, Müller never asked other people to help meet his needs. Extreme financial pressures only motivated him to spend more time in intimate conversation with God.

Listen to what Müller said about his times alone with God: "I begin to meditate on the New Testament early in the mornings. . . . Invariably, I have found that . . . after so many minutes of meditation, my soul is guided to confession, or to give thanks, or to intercede, or to make a request. So, even when you couldn't say that I had given myself to prayer, but rather to meditation, nevertheless, it turned out that almost immediately the meditation turned into prayer."

As God's Word spoke to Müller's heart, he naturally responded back to God in prayer. He enjoyed intimate fellowship with his Lord.

Communication is the key to any relationship. Our relationship with God can grow only as we communicate our adoration, confession, petition, intercession, and thanksgiving to Him through prayer, and as we listen to His voice through the daily study of His Word.

How well do you know God? How intimate is your relationship with Him? Müller could come to God, ask Him for five pounds, and know his heavenly Father would somehow supply his need. Could you ask God for that, or are you only an acquaintance?

TO PONDER

• As a child of God, how well do you know your heavenly Father? How well do you want to know Him?

TO PURSUE

• During your next time of prayer, begin by meditating on a passage of Scripture. Then pray to God, listening to what He is saying to you from that Bible passage.

Accepting the
Bible's Authority

The authority of Scripture is one of the oldest and most discussed questions of humankind. It is also one of the most important for us to consider today. People often prove their spiritual condition by their attitude toward the Bible.

Several years ago I had the opportunity to meet with about a dozen ministers near a city where I was involved in a crusade. To say I was shocked by our discussion may be a bit too strong, but I was certainly surprised by the serious differences of opinion we had on some basic questions. At least half of these ministers did not accept the Bible as the authoritative Word of God!

Several said they believed some Scripture passages were erroneous. Even more astonishing was their admission that when they are uncomfortable with portions of the Bible, they rationalize away such portions as "unscientific."

Is it any wonder that in certain parts of the world the Christian church staggers? Who wants to listen to ministers who don't believe the Bible is the Word of God? Where is their authority? Where do you draw the line between which passages of the Bible are inspired by God and which are not?

When I hear people who profess to be Christians questioning whether the Bible is God's Word, I can't help but wonder if Christians today worship too small a God. After all, if God is God, then couldn't He write a Book that is without error? Of course He could, and He did!

Paul could confidently tell Timothy, "Continue in what you have learned and have become convinced of, because you know those from whom you learned it, and how from infancy you have known the holy Scriptures, which are able to make you wise for salvation through faith in Christ Jesus" (2 Timothy 3:14–15). Why could Paul say that? Because all Scripture is inspired by God; it is authoritative because it is *God's* Word, not man's.

Peter could write, "We did not follow cleverly invented stories when we told you about the power and coming of our Lord Jesus Christ, but we were eyewitnesses of his majesty" (2 Peter 1:16).

The Bible has the ring of authenticity. No other book has this divine stamp of approval.

Arthur T. Pierson, a noted Bible expositor, explained the Bible's uniqueness this way: "From all human oracles, however self-confident, we turn at last to the inspired Word, where instead of ambiguous and untrustworthy utterances, we find teachings distinct and definite, authoritative and infallible." We can trust God's Word!

If God couldn't write a book that is perfect, then why should you or I trust such a God with our salvation? I am not saying that belief in inspiration is necessary for salvation, but I am saying that to experience authority and power and fellowship with God in our Christian walk, we must accept the Bible as God's Word.

Belief in the full authority of Scripture is vital to living an authentic and victorious Christian life. Only through such faith can we experience the joy of being God's children.

TO PONDER

• Until now, how have you viewed the Bible? Have you accepted Scripture as fully authoritative, infallible, and inspired by the Lord? Why or why not?

TO PURSUE

• Make a list of reasons why you do (or don't) believe in the authority of Scripture. If you have specific questions about the Bible's infallibility or inspiration, talk with your pastor. Or mail them to me. I'll be glad to correspond with you.

Reaffirming the Bible's Authority

Many people today attack the authority of God's Word. They throw out certain passages and question many others. How should we respond to such attacks?

Charles Spurgeon responded this way: "Defend the Word of God? Might as well defend a lion." It doesn't need any defense. We can confidently follow the footsteps of godly men and women throughout the ages in acknowledging the Bible's authority.

Jesus Christ Himself recognized the Scriptures as God's Word. He made a point of quoting supposedly controversial or "hard-to-believe" passages in the Old Testament just to attest to their historical accuracy. The Lord referred to the creation story (Matthew 19:4–6; Mark 10:2–9; 13:19), Noah and the flood (Matthew 24:36–39; Luke 17:26–27), and Lot and the cities of Sodom and Gomorrah (Matthew 10:15; Luke 10:12; 17:28–30).

Jesus even referred to the Old Testament account of Jonah (Matthew 12:40–41; 16:4). Many people today laugh at the story of Jonah and shrug it off as a fairy tale or bedtime story for little children. Why? Because according to what knowledge they have about science, it is impossible for a whale to swallow a man and then vomit him alive out of his belly after three days.

First of all, the Bible doesn't say Jonah was swallowed by a whale, but rather by a great fish (Jonah 1:17). More importantly, the historical account is recorded in the Bible, and Jesus said it happened. If Jesus believed it, why shouldn't we believe it too?

The Bible clearly states, "All Scripture is God-breathed" (2 Timothy 3:16). John R.W. Stott explains the importance of this declaration for us this way: "The meaning then is not that God breathed into the writings to give them their special character, but that what was written by men was breathed by God. He spoke through them. These were his spokesmen."

The very words of Scripture are inspired by God. Someone has said, "You can as easily have music without notes, or mathematics without figures, as thoughts without words." Inspiration applies to every part of the Bible and to the Bible as a whole—not just to the "thoughts" it conveys to a reader.

Jesus said, "I tell you the truth, until heaven and earth disappear, not the smallest letter, not the least stroke of a pen, will by any means disappear from the Law until everything is accomplished" (Matthew 5:18). He guarantees even the most minute parts of it!

The early church fathers also asserted the authority of the Bible. Augustine declared, "Let us therefore yield ourselves and bow to the authority of the Holy Scriptures, which can neither err nor deceive."

Why should we cower before the attacks of certain critics of the Bible? As God's children, we need submit only to Him and His authoritative Word. Scripture is the standard by which we should measure everything else.

TO PONDER

• Have you ever heard someone attack the authority of the Bible? How do you feel about such attacks? How do you respond?

• If Scripture *is* God's Word, what are the implications?

TO PURSUE

• In prayer, make a commitment to take God at His Word. Let the Lord know you will believe wholeheartedly what He says and obey gladly what He commands.

Living the
Word of Life

Why was the Bible written?

To explain the complexities of human government? To critique certain theories of economics? To teach us the wonders of astronomy?

The primary purpose of the Bible is not to tell us how the heavens go, but how to go to heaven. The Bible's great message is that God desires to transform the lives of His children through His Word, preparing them for eternity with Him in glory.

God's Word has power to transform individuals from condemned sinners to redeemed believers. I know this personally, because a British gentleman named Frank Chandler brought me to saving faith in Jesus Christ by reading Romans 10:9–10 to me.

I was only twelve years old when I sincerely committed my life to Christ through prayer, but from that moment on I knew I was a child of God. I knew I was going to heaven when I died. Christ had paid for my sins by His death on the cross.

Conversion—the transformation of an individual from a sinner to a child of God—is impossible apart from God's Word. Missionaries brought God's saving Word to Argentina, where I grew up. My father is in heaven because of their work. My grandmother is in heaven because of their work. Millions of people around the world, including myself, thank God for the missionaries who brought God's Word.

The Bible has the power to transform anyone, anywhere—the high or low, the rich or poor, the educated or illiterate. I even have had the privilege of seeing several heads of state come to know Christ personally, including the president of a certain country in South America.

He told me, "Palau, I'm a military man. I have done things I could never tell you about. If you knew what I was really like, you would never say God loves me."

I replied, "I don't want you to tell me. Whatever you've done, Jesus Christ came to save and transform men and women just like you." Even though he was a gentleman of high position and military rank, he bowed his head and opened his heart to the Lord Jesus right there in his presidential office.

Even when this president lost his office two years later during a revolution, he continued to go on for the Lord. He later said, "My life has been changed since the day I gave my life to Christ."

I have seen the Word of God transform the lives of many, many people: the secretary of a national communist party . . . an illiterate janitor . . . a princess in Britain . . . the prime minister of a South Pacific nation . . . the New York City Marathon women's record holder . . . an ex-convict who trusted Jesus Christ "on the air" during a live, call-in television program . . . one of the best-known actresses in El Salvador . . . an East Coast disk jockey . . . a night club singer . . . a high school student now studying at MIT . . . punk rockers in Poland . . . a banker's daughter, sixteen, pregnant out of wedlock . . . mayors of several cities . . . gang members . . . spiritists . . . couples in the process of filing for divorce . . . a military general's wife . . . ambassadors . . . agnostics . . . atheists . . . Hindus . . . Buddhists . . . Muslims . . . and a good number of nominal "Christians."

The Bible has the power to save and then transform anyone, anywhere. That transforming work is known as *sanctification*. God's Word frees us from sin, cleanses us, and makes us holy in our walk before God.

The Lord Jesus prayed to His Father in the Garden of Gethsemane, "Sanctify them by the truth; your word is truth" (John 17:17). His Word cleanses us (John 15:3).

It isn't enough to know the Scriptures "are able to make you wise for salvation through faith in Christ Jesus" (2 Timothy 3:15). Paul goes on to say in verse 16, "All Scripture is God-breathed *and is useful for teaching, rebuking, correcting and training in righteousness*" (italics added).

The Word immediately points out the sin spots on the altar of our soul. Dusty Bibles, however, lead to dirty lives.

TO PONDER

• What impact has Scripture made in your heart and home? How would your life be different without God's Word?

• How much of the Bible have you read? Did you know that by investing only fifteen minutes a day, you could read God's Word from cover to cover, like any other book, in a year?

TO PURSUE

• Select a good reading Bible, in a version you understand and respect, that you can highlight or underline. Read at least one chapter today and every day.

• If you plan to buy a new reading Bible, I recommend *The One Year Bible* (Tyndale), available in several versions.

Reading God's
Daily Bread

One of my earliest memories is of sneaking out of bed early in the morning to watch my father kneel, pray, and read the Bible before going to work. That deeply impressed me as a child.

Every day my dad read a chapter from Proverbs, since it has thirty-one chapters and most months have thirty-one days. I still try to practice his suggestion today. In spite of all my other Bible studying and reading, I start the day with one chapter from Proverbs. And I have learned to do it on my knees.

Robert Murray McCheyne is another godly man whose love for the Bible and devotion to God has marked my life and ministry.

Born in 1813 in Edinburgh, Scotland, McCheyne died at the age of twenty-nine. Yet in his short lifetime, because of his holiness, humility, and anxious efforts to save souls, he made a lasting impression on society.

The need for personal holiness before God so impressed McCheyne that he wrote, "According to your holiness, so shall be your success. . . . A holy man is an awesome weapon in the hand of God."

Many factors make a lasting impact for good on a community or nation. But holiness among the people of God, particularly among the leadership, is fundamental. Sin—a lack of holiness—grieves the Holy Spirit and hinders His work. Scripture warns, "Do not grieve the Holy Spirit" (Ephesians 4:30) and "Do not put out the Spirit's fire" (1 Thessalonians 5:19).

On the other hand, Scripture exhorts us, "Be filled with the Spirit" (Ephesians 5:18). To be filled with the Spirit is a command, a duty, and a privilege for the Christian. To be filled with the Spirit means to be walking in His light and to be controlled by the indwelling Lord. To do this we must spend time each day reading and meditating on the Bible, filling our minds and hearts with the life-changing, inspired Word of God (Colossians 3:16).

To encourage holy, Spirit-filled living among his congregation, McCheyne developed and published a Bible reading guide entitled *Daily Bread*. He urged fellow believers to read the Holy Scripture "in all its breadth."

In many nations today McCheyne's *Daily Bread* guide is widely used among Christians who are serious about knowing and obeying God's Word. The guide suggests two short readings for each morning and evening, and covers the entire Bible in one year.

How about you? Have you disciplined yourself to read the Bible each day? If not, start today! Like my dad, begin in the book of Proverbs, and then systematically read the entire Bible each year.

Why let another day go by without partaking of your daily bread?

TO PONDER

• Are you currently spending time every day reading at least one chapter of the Bible? If not, how often *are* you reading God's Word?

• If you spent time daily in Scripture, what impact could it make on your life? On the lives of others around you?

TO PURSUE

• Select a specific, realistic plan for reading a portion of God's Word each day.

• To receive a free copy of Robert Murray McCheyne's Bible reading guide, write to Luis Palau, "Daily Bread" Offer, P.O. Box 1173, Portland, Oregon 97207.

Studying the
Bible for Yourself

Do you enjoy studying the Bible on your own? Are you satisfied with your ability to apply biblical truths to daily living?

Christians sometimes neglect to study God's Word because they lack a simple, practical method that makes Bible study come alive for them. As God's children, we cannot grow and mature spiritually, however, unless we eat regularly from the Bread of Life.

One Christian leader stated, "I cannot too greatly emphasize the importance and value of Bible study . . . in these days of uncertainties, when men and women are apt to decide questions from the standpoint of expediency rather than on the eternal principles laid down by God Himself."

Bible study starts with *observation*. Our observations of any object, including the Bible, are directed by the nature of the object to be studied. We observe stars by looking at them through a telescope night after night. We observe animals' behavior by watching them over a long period of time in their natural habitat. We observe the Bible as we would any book—by reading it carefully and frequently.

Noted Bible teacher Dr. James M. Gray declared, "There is only one law of Bible study, and that is to read the Book, and when you have read it, to read it again, and then sit down and read it again, and then sit down and read it once more, and by and by you will come to *know* the Book."

Read the book of the Bible you are studying in one sitting. The gospel of John and 2 Corinthians are good books to study at first. Get a clear impression of the book as a whole. Disregard chapter and verse divisions. Read it again and again, occasionally using various translations to better grasp its message. Ask probing questions: Who? What? When? Where? Why? How?

After observing the text, *interpretation* follows. We must guard against allowing our presuppositions to bias our interpretation. Pray for the Spirit's enlightening; apart from His illumination, proper understanding is elusive (1 John 2:20, 27).

Examine the context of the passage you are interpreting. Also compare the passage with parallel accounts and cross-references.

Charles Spurgeon remarked, "Nowadays we hear men tear a simple sentence of Scripture from its connection and cry, 'Eureka! Eureka!' as if they had found a new truth; and yet they have not found a true diamond, but a piece of broken glass."

The best Bible commentary is the Bible itself. But Bible handbooks and dictionaries and a good atlas help us better understand biblical lands, customs, and history. Consult them when needed, being careful not to spend a great deal of time reading about the Bible without ever turning to God's Word for yourself.

Finally, the study of God's Word must lead to its *application* to your life. You haven't done this unless it changes your behavior. Relate the Bible to all areas of your life—your strengths and weaknesses, attitudes and actions. What does it say to you as a parent or child, husband or wife, friend or neighbor, employee or employer?

James tells us, "Do not merely listen to the word, and so deceive yourselves. Do what it says" (James 1:22).

Obey the Word by prayerfully meditating on it with the goal of better understanding and applying it.

Observation. Interpretation. Application. These three simple steps are the keys that open the door for exciting Bible study!

TO PONDER

• Do you have a simple, practical method for studying God's Word? What method do you use? Does it help you *apply* the Bible to your life?

TO PURSUE

• Don't just read Scripture. After you finish your Bible reading, chew on God's Word and digest it for a few minutes. Determine, *What does this passage teach? What does it mean? How does this apply to me?*

Memorizing
God's Word

Warning: *Authorities have determined that Scripture memorization may be hazardous to your spiritual health.*

Dawson Trotman, founder of The Navigators, once asked a young man how much Scripture he knew. The serviceman said he had memorized 1,500 verses.

"You mean you could quote 1,500 verses to me right now?" Trotman asked incredulously.

"That's right," the young man said with obvious pride.

Trotman replied, "I wish you could quote only five verses—*but live them!*" This young man had only head knowledge of Scripture, not heart application.

Many years ago the village priest in Kalonovaka, Russia, took a special liking to a pug-nosed lad who recited his Scriptures with proper piety. By offering various inducements, the priest managed to teach the boy the four Gospels, which he recited nonstop in church one day.

Sixty years later he still liked to recite Scriptures, but in a context that would have horrified the old priest. The prize pupil who memorized so much of the Bible was Nikita Khrushchev, former premier of the Soviet Union!

John W. Alexander, former president of InterVarsity Christian Fellowship, gives us this warning: "There is little merit inherent in the mere process of memorizing Scripture. One could memorize voluminous portions and be an atheist. Satan memorized enough to use it to tempt Jesus."

Alexander goes on to add, however, "Memorizing *is* helpful when we yearn for Scripture to energize our whole lives."

Warning: *Authorities also have determined that Scripture memorization can greatly enhance your spiritual vitality.*

What makes the difference between superficial and beneficial Scripture memorization? I believe it is *prayerful meditation.*
Memorization in itself may sharpen our intellectual capacities, but that's about all. Memorization with a view to meditation helps us think straight in a crooked world.

The Bible says, "Whatever is true, whatever is noble, whatever is right, whatever is pure, whatever is lovely, whatever is admirable—if anything is excellent or praiseworthy—think about such things" (Philippians 4:8).

How can we think on what is pure when we are confronted daily with impurity? By purposefully meditating on God's Word.

We can't read the Bible all day, but we can always meditate on passages of Scripture—if we have memorized them. After twenty-four hours, research shows, we accurately remember five percent of what we hear, fifteen percent of what we read, thirty-five percent of what we study, but one hundred percent of what we memorize.

Let me suggest five tips for memorizing Scripture I think you will find helpful.

1. Read the verse out loud at least ten times.
2. Write it out on a 3"x5" card, thinking about each word.
3. Practice quoting it (it should be easy by now).
4. Meditate on it throughout the day and review it on subsequent days.
5. Share the verse with other people as you converse together.

I strongly encourage you to start memorizing Scripture passages and meditating on them. But let me warn you: It may change your life!

TO PONDER

• When life slows down for a minute, what do you tend to think about? Do you struggle with lustful thoughts, worry, pride, envy?

• What difference would it make if you hid God's Word in your heart?

TO PURSUE

• If you don't already have a Scripture memory plan, proceed immediately to Habit 13.

HABIT 13

Scripture Passages
That Can Change
Your Life

If you don't have an established Scripture memorization plan, start with the verses I have listed below. I have memorized and meditated on all of these passages, and they have made a significant difference in my life. They can change your life as well!

New Birth
1. Salvation—John 3:16
2. New life—2 Corinthians 5:17
3. Identity as God's child—1 John 3:1–2
4. God lives in you—1 Corinthians 6:19–20
5. Baptized into one body—1 Corinthians 12:13

God
6. Christ as the Word—John 1:1–2
7. The Spirit of God—John 15:26
8. Counselor—John 14:16–17
9. God's strength—Ephesians 6:10–11

Family
10. Wives—Ephesians 5:22
11. Husbands—Ephesians 5:25
12. Children—Ephesians 6:1–3
13. Parents—Ephesians 6:4

Growth
14. Temptation—1 Corinthians 10:13
15. Confession and forgiveness—1 John 1:9
16. Prayer—John 14:13–14
17. Meeting together—Hebrews 10:24–25

18. Loving one another—John 13:34–35
19. Freedom from legalism—Colossians 2:20–22

God's Word
20. Authority—2 Peter 1:20–21
21. Purpose—2 Timothy 3:16–17
22. For our purity—Psalm 119:9–11

Victory
23. Walk in the Spirit—Galatians 5:16–18
24. Dedication and transformation—Romans 12:1–2
25. Victory through the cross—Galatians 2:20
26. The fruit of the Spirit—Galatians 5:22–23
27. The Great Commission—Matthew 28:18–20
28. Death and resurrection in Christ—Romans 6:3–4

The Future
29. Eternal condemnation—Revelation 21:8
30. Heaven—John 14:1–3

Discipline yourself to learn one verse or short passage every week (memorize faster if you wish). *Check off each verse as you learn it.*

But don't stop there! Meditate on these verses. Say them over in your mind occasionally throughout the day. Keep asking, *So what? What difference should this make in my life?*

Pray that you will be able to hide each verse not only in your head, but also in your heart so God can use it to change your life (Psalm 119:11). Ask God to help you hear what He is trying to say to you through His Word.

TO PONDER

• How many verses of Scripture do you know by heart? How many can you quote right now, without any review, by memory? With a little discipline, how many could you learn in the next six months?

TO PURSUE

• Start small: (re)memorize John 3:16 this week from your reading Bible, whatever translation it is. Next week, (re)learn 2 Corinthians 5:17. Get into the habit of reviewing the Scripture verses you already know. Then, each week, hide one more verse in your heart.

PART TWO

Cultivating Dependence
as God's Pilgrim

The trials and temptations we encounter as pilgrims passing through this world prompt us to depend upon God and His Word all the more.

■ *Habit*

Claiming God's Promises for Yourself

As you have read and studied, memorized and meditated on various passages in the Bible, what sections have seemed the most difficult to believe?

Prophecy? Narrative portions? Doctrinal passages? Or God's promises?

Many Christians have the most problem believing the promises of God. Oh, they sound nice, and sometimes they even cheer us up. But we wonder, *Are they really true?* Unconsciously, at least, we question whether or not God keeps His promises.

D.L. Moody confidently stated, "God never made a promise that was too good to be true." Think about that!

In the Old Testament we read, "Not one of all the Lord's good promises to the house of Israel failed; every one was fulfilled" (Joshua 21:45; compare 23:14–15). Solomon later declared, "Praise be to the Lord, who has given rest to his people Israel just as he promised. Not one word has failed of all the good promises he gave through his servant Moses" (1 Kings 8:56).

None of God's promises have ever failed! The only absolutes we can proclaim are those found in God's Word. The Bible testifies of things beyond what man knows or can learn apart from God's revelation.

God has gone on record many times throughout His authoritative Word and has given us—His pilgrims passing through this world—"very great and precious promises" (2 Peter 1:4).

Some of His promises were made specifically to an individual (Joshua 14:9), a group (Deuteronomy 15:18), or a nation (Haggai 1:13). We must be careful not to claim haphazardly promises intended for someone else!

Many Old Testament promises, thankfully, are repeated in the New Testament and are ours to claim today. God promised Joshua, "I will never leave you or forsake you" (Joshua 1:5). In Hebrews 13:5 God transfers that promise to us as Christians.

Charles Spurgeon stated, "O man, I beseech you, do not treat God's promises as if they were curiosities for a museum; but believe them and use them." We appropriate God's promises by learning them (through study and memorization), by seeing our need for them (through meditation), and by giving God time to work them out in our daily experience (through application).

J.I. Packer said, "God teaches the believer to value His promised gifts by making him wait for them, and compelling him to pray persistently for them, before He bestows them."

God has promised to meet our every need. But we must ask for His provision. Christ says, "Ask and it will be given to you; seek and you will find; knock and the door will be opened to you" (Matthew 7:7).

Any of God's promises that we can claim in Jesus' name are guaranteed and will be performed for us by God for His glory (John 14:13–14; 2 Corinthians 1:20).

What is the need of your heart today? The Lord has promised to meet that need! Simply take Him at His Word.

TO PONDER

• What is one of your favorite Bible promises? Why is it one of your favorites? How has God used that promise in your life?

• What is one of your biggest needs at the moment? How has God promised in His Word to meet that need? In which verse(s)?

TO PURSUE

• Select a new promise of God to memorize and meditate on this week. Or review an old favorite that speaks to a current need.

• If you don't already have a Bible promise book, look for one the next time you visit your local Christian bookstore.

Claiming God's Promises
When We Hurt

Several years ago a submarine sank, with all its crew, off the Atlantic coast of North America. When the vessel was eventually located, divers were sent down to assess the damage and the possibility of salvaging the wreck.

As the divers neared the hull of the vessel, they were surprised to hear the pounding of a message in Morse code. It was evident someone actually was alive inside the submarine. The message was a frantic question beat against the walls of the aquatic tomb: "Is there hope? Is there hope?"

You and I ponder that same question when a particular problem or tragedy strikes us. Who, after all, is totally free in this life from the crushing pain of losing a loved one, or the frustration of unemployment, or the anguish of a fragmented home, or any of a hundred other problems?

We feel trapped and submerged by the weight of our circumstances and wonder, "Is there hope? Is there really any hope of overcoming this problem?"

We often remember Romans 8:28 in such times: "We know that in all things God works for the good of those who love him, who have been called according to his purpose." Vance Havner commented, "Paul did not say, 'We understand how all things work together for good'; he said, 'We *know* that they do.' " That promise is a solid anchor when the storms of life beat heavily against us.

The apostle Paul had claimed that very promise many times before he ever penned his famous letter to the Romans. As one of God's pilgrims passing through this world, he knew what it was to suffer hardship, persecution, indifference, betrayal, loneliness, stonings, beatings, shipwreck, nakedness, destitution, sleeplessness, and immense pressure.

What kept Paul from going under? I believe it was his utter confidence in the God who promises to sustain us no matter what. At the end of his life he could say, "I know whom I have believed, and am convinced that he is able to guard what I have entrusted to him for that day" (2 Timothy 1:12). What had Paul entrusted to God? His very life!

In the Old Testament we read, "You will keep in perfect peace him whose mind is steadfast, because he trusts in you" (Isaiah 26:3). That promise applies to us even today, as the New Testament repeatedly affirms.

Are you facing a difficult problem today? Commit yourself anew to the Lord. Then take the words of Philippians 4:6–7 to heart: "Do not be anxious about anything, but in everything, by prayer and petition, with thanksgiving, present your requests to God. And the peace of God, which transcends all understanding, will guard your hearts and your minds in Christ Jesus."

When the storms of life seem overwhelming, God wants us to experience His perfect peace.

O Father, I praise You that You understand my every sorrow and tear. I acknowledge my insufficiency to handle life's problems in my own strength. I gladly acknowledge my dependence upon You. May Your grace abound to meet my deepest needs. Sustain me as I wait upon You. Fill my heart with Your peace that passes all understanding. Thank You for Your rich provision for me this day. Amen.

TO PONDER

• How would you describe your circumstances today?

• Think back to a time when the storms of life seemed to be beating especially heavily upon you. What was your response? What was God's response?

TO PURSUE

• Use the above prayer right now, in your own words, to affirm your dependence upon God, whatever the circumstances.

Understanding Why
God Allows Suffering

A philosopher from Paris once commented, "God is dead. Marx is dead. And I don't feel so good myself." His attitude illustrates the pessimism rampant in our culture today.

If there really is a God, people wonder, *why has He allowed so much suffering in the world?*

Many Christians honestly struggle with that same question. Only by turning to the Bible can we begin to understand the problem of suffering in this life.

Basically, there are four types of suffering. The first type is that which comes as the result of natural disasters, such as an earthquake or a hurricane. The suffering that results from these disasters happens to both the righteous and unrighteous (Matthew 5:45).

A second type of suffering can be called man's inhumanity to man. War would be classified under this type of suffering. Because of humanity's greed and pride, people try to hurt other people (James 4:1–2).

A third type of suffering is best seen in the life of Job in the Old Testament; it came as a result of Satan's attack on him. After receiving permission from God, Satan moved in and caused incredible suffering to Job and his family.

A fourth type of suffering is that which comes as a result of our own erroneous actions. For example, if I walk off the roof of my office and fall to the ground, breaking my leg, I am suffering because I broke God's law of gravity. We also suffer when we break God's *moral* laws.

Much suffering can be traced to the evil choices we make. Some, but not all, suffering is allowed by God as a punishment for sin. Often God simply forces us to live with the consequences of our actions (Galatians 6:7–8).

Whenever people break God's laws, others are bound to suffer as well. I refer you to the story of Achan in Joshua 7. When he coveted and took some of the spoil from the battle of Jericho, Achan cost the lives of thirty-six men in battle against Ai. It is inevitable that others will suffer in the wake of an individual's disobedience.

How we respond to suffering—whether or not we brought it on ourselves—is going to make us or break us as Christian pilgrims. Circumstances often do more to reveal our character than to shape it. But by properly responding to trials, we can develop patience and proven character (Romans 5:3–4).

Problems, stress, calamity, or the death of a loved one often cause us to search ourselves for any sin in our lives (see 1 Kings 17:18). Pain plants the flag of truth in a heavy heart. But we must be cautious not to let Satan overwhelm us with excessive and false guilt or grief (2 Corinthians 2:7). Job's wife told him to curse God and die. He refused to give up and remained faithful to the Lord. Notice that in the end God gave him all he had before and even more (Job 42:10–17).

Instead of looking at our circumstances, we need to keep our eyes on Jesus Christ, the source of life. He will bring us through whatever situation we face, and as a result we will be stronger Christians, better able to serve Him because of our trials.

In a day of pessimism and suffering we can say with the psalmist, "The Lord is with me; I will not be afraid. What can man do to me?" (Psalm 118:6). The Lord Himself, as the great Sufferer, is our comfort and hope in troubled times.

TO PONDER

• To what degree have you experienced the first kind of suffering described above? The second? The third? The fourth?

• Are you currently going through a trial? What kind of trial is it? What has been your response so far?

TO PURSUE

• This week memorize and meditate on Psalm 118:6 and Hebrews 13:5–6, verses which have been an encouragement to me and to many others during times of trial.

Maintaining a
Proper Perspective

Did you know a single cup of coffee contains enough moisture to blanket your entire neighborhood with fog fifty feet thick?

It's amazing how such a small amount of water—spread out so thinly—can hinder our vision almost completely.

We tend to get upset when fog hinders our pilgrimage, but we forget the sun is still shining overhead, burning it away. Why do we get upset? Because we fail to maintain a proper perspective.

British statesman William Wilberforce once commented, "The objects of the present life fill the human eye with a false magnification because of their immediacy." Problems and concerns often act like fog to obscure our present situation. They keep us from seeing things in proper perspective.

Psychologists tell us that forty-five percent of what we worry about is past, and forty-five percent is future. (Thirty percent concerns our health alone!) Only one in every ten things we worry about will ever come to pass—and we usually cannot do anything about it anyway.

No wonder Jesus Christ tells us, "Do not worry about tomorrow, for tomorrow will worry about itself" (Matthew 6:34). The Bible also says, "Do not be anxious about anything" (Philippians 4:6). We worry whenever we fail to maintain a true perspective of our circumstances.

Sometimes we treat problems and trials as if we were on a television commercial. We rush around thinking we have to solve everything in thirty seconds. When we can't, we panic.

We try every option we can think of to overcome our problems and difficulties. When none of them works, we reluctantly turn to God as a last resort.

But there are no emergencies in heaven. God is aware of our problems (Exodus 3:7; 1 Peter 5:7). He did not create us to be self-sufficient to meet our needs. He created us to depend on Him. A.W. Tozer wrote, "The man who comes to a right belief about God is relieved of ten thousand temporal problems, for he sees at once that these have to do with matters which at the most cannot concern him for very long."

Do you face a difficult situation, my friend? Has your way been covered by a heavy fog? God has not allowed this situation to come into your life to discourage or defeat you. Every trial you and I face is an opportunity for God to demonstrate who He is to us—the One we can always depend upon, no matter what.

King Hezekiah saw God demonstrate His care for him in a dramatic way. Meditate on Isaiah 37 and record the steps that King Hezekiah took when faced with a serious problem. Then compare your list with mine below.

1. Hezekiah acknowledged that he had a problem (37:1).
2. He sought to know what God's Word said about his problem (37:2–7).
3. He didn't allow anything to distort his perspective (37:8–13).
4. He prayed to God—first worshiping Him, then presenting his request, and finally asking that God would be glorified (37:14–20).

Use these same steps when you face a difficulty or trial. Remember, it is in the hard places that we get to know Him better.

TO PONDER

- Do you tend to have a problem with worry?
- What have you been worried about lately? Health? Work? Finances? Marriage? Family? Church? National issues?

TO PURSUE

- Review Isaiah 37:1–20, making brief notes in the margin of your Bible about how King Hezekiah responded during a time of crisis. Use those same steps to address areas of personal concern.

Facing Death

One of the most difficult trials each of us will face is the death of a loved one. It is hard to keep things in perspective when death strikes so close to home, isn't it?

Modern man strives frantically to prolong life and overcome death's power. Physicians use extraordinary measures to keep the sick and dying alive just a little longer through wonder drugs, organ transplants, and sophisticated machinery. That was certainly the case when my nephew, Kenneth, was dying of AIDS several years ago.

But death continues harvesting its fruit without prejudice toward age, race, social level, or education. Death continues to be cynical, cruel, and real. No one escapes its cold fingers. Our appointment is sure. Neither money, fame, nor intelligence exempt us from death; everyone succumbs.

How should we respond as believers when a dearly loved Christian relative or friend dies?

Shortly before my father died he suddenly sat up in bed and sang a chorus about heaven. Then he fell back on his pillow and said, "I'm going to be with Jesus, which is far better."

My father had committed his life to Jesus Christ nine years earlier and was confident he would spend eternity with the Lord. He was thirty-six years old when he went to glory; I was only ten at the time.

He died just hours before I returned home from a term at boarding school. I had no way of knowing what had happened as I stepped off the train that day and ran home. But as I neared my house I could hear weeping.

My relatives tried to intercept me as I ran through the gate and up to the house; I brushed past them and was in the door before my mother even knew I was back. Tears filled my eyes when I saw my father's expired body lying in front of me.

I felt devastated by my father's death. My world seemed shattered and confused. I was angry at everything and everybody. *It isn't fair,* I thought. *Why couldn't my dad die in old age like other dads?*

A missionary delivered the message before my father's burial the next morning. It was only then I felt complete assurance that my father was in heaven.

Oh, I still missed my dad terribly. I still felt the pangs of grief. But I rested in the hope that one day, when my pilgrimage is over, I will see him again.

Grief is a normal part of facing the death of a loved one. We do grieve at the death of other believers, but not as those who have no hope (1 Thessalonians 4:13).

Jesus gives us these words of comfort: "Do not let your hearts be troubled. Trust in God; trust also in me. In my Father's house are many rooms; if it were not so, I would have told you. I am going there to prepare a place for you. And if I go and prepare a place for you, I will come back and take you to be with me that you also may be where I am" (John 14:1–3). That is our blessed hope as believers!

Yes, the grieving process is absolutely normal for our emotional and physical well-being. But as Christians we do not have to be swallowed up in that grief, or allow anger or bitterness to take root in our hearts.

We can face death with hope, realizing it is not the end. Death is merely earth's door to heaven.

TO PONDER

• Has anyone close to you died? Who? Did he or she know the Lord? When did he or she die, and how did you respond?

TO PURSUE

• If you are still grieving for a loved one who has died, take a few minutes to tell the Lord about your grief and reaffirm your trust in Him.

Beyond Death's Door

Death haunts humankind. Poets, philosophers, and other writers throughout the ages have sought to explain, understand, and cope with death.

Ernest Hemingway, the famous author, was obsessed with the reality of death. His father, an intellectual, had killed himself when Hemingway was a young man. As a result, Hemingway wanted to demonstrate to all humanity that he feared neither life nor death. Ironically, when he was sixty-one years old, he committed suicide in a moment of rage and human weakness.

The Bible recognizes the inevitability of physical death. In Hebrews 9:27 we read, "Man is destined to die." In a sense, everyone is terminally ill. Unless Christ returns in our lifetime, our pilgrimage through this world will end in death.

Longfellow succinctly observed, "The young may die, and the old must." Physically death is the most stubborn and persistent enemy of humanity. But it is not the most dangerous foe.

The Bible distinguishes between physical death (which everyone eventually faces) and spiritual death (which everyone initially experiences). Death basically means separation from something or someone. It implies loneliness. A person begins life separated from God and spiritually dead because of his or her sin.

Sartre, the famous French existential philosopher, accurately observed, "Man is alone." Apart from a personal relationship with God and commitment to Him, every human being is spiritually dead and very much alone.

The Bible also mentions eternal death or "the second death" (Revelation 20:14). This is eternal, irreversible separation from God. Anyone who refuses to commit one's life to Jesus Christ during his or her lifetime here on earth will experience this eternal death.

Physical death clearly is *not* the end of our existence. The question is where you and I will spend eternity—in heaven or hell? There is no other option. The reality of death and hell should motivate Christians to share the gospel of Jesus Christ with the unconverted.

Approximately one-quarter million people die each day around the world. Most pass into a Christless eternity. History frequently records their agonizing last words when they realize that by rejecting Christ they are left without hope.

Francois Voltaire, the noted French infidel, once stated, "In twenty years, Christianity will be no more. My single hand shall destroy the edifice it took twelve apostles to rear." Yet when he faced death he cried, "I am abandoned by God and man!" Voltaire's doctor expressed astonishment at the emotional torment his patient experienced before passing into eternity.

In contrast, the great evangelist John Wesley declared on his deathbed, "The best of all is, God is with me!" He finished his pilgrimage satisfied and content to be in the presence of his Lord.

Death need not haunt us as Christians. If we have committed our lives to Jesus Christ, we have a glorious future awaiting us beyond death's door.

TO PONDER

• If you discovered you had only six weeks to live, would you be afraid of the thought of dying? Why or why not?

• If the Lord doesn't return first, at the end of your life what do you want to say as your last words?

TO PURSUE

• Ask the Lord to give you the grace to love those who don't know Him yet, and the courage to tell them about your Savior.

Reason for Living

More than eleven thousand people tried to commit suicide during the past twenty-four hours. According to a report from the United Nations, one thousand of these people succeeded in taking their lives. And a high percentage of these suicides were among young people.

Several years ago a high school friend of one of my sons put a gun to his head and shot himself. He was sixteen, the son of a wealthy and notable doctor. He had not been exhibiting any unusual signs of stress. But one day he came home from school and began calling some of his classmates to tell them he was going to kill himself.

"The guys didn't believe him," my son told me. "They thought he was joking." An hour later this young man proved they were wrong. Why? Partially because his friends failed to respond properly when he called them. They apparently believed several myths about suicide.

One popular myth about suicide is that if someone talks about killing himself, he won't really do it. The fact is that a person *does* talk about it, usually with up to ten people, before attempting to take his own life. That is exactly what my son's friend did.

Sometimes people simply write a note and then kill themselves, but most people talk about it first. They may have specific plans to carry out the suicide, but they want to be rescued instead. Perhaps that is why most suicide attempts, though serious, are not fatal. People just want to know someone cares about them. Suicide is their immature, impulsive way to get that attention.

Another myth about suicide is that if you mention the word *suicide* to someone who you notice is emotionally distraught or unstable, you will put the thought in his or her mind. That is false. When my son's classmate told several friends he was going to kill himself, they should have seriously questioned him about his suicidal intentions, not laughed as if he were joking.

Suicides are increasing at alarming rates among all classes and types of people. One study on suicide revealed this surprising fact: Psychiatrists have the highest suicide rate of any professional group. And they are the ones who are supposed to help those without hope!

Many people readily turn to Christians when they are contemplating suicide. If a friend or acquaintance causes you to think he or she may be suicidal, make time to see that person as soon as possible.

Don't be fooled by the myths about suicide. Maybe your friend has never even thought about suicide. But don't be afraid to ask him or her about it.

If your friend says he is thinking about killing himself, take him seriously and act quickly to get him to someone who can help him. Don't let him out of your sight, especially if he has a specific plan for killing himself (method, place, time). Suicide is no joking matter.

Why do people attempt suicide? There are many reasons: seeking to get attention, desiring to join a dead relative, anger that is internalized, loss of meaning in life, poor health, loneliness.

Make it a priority to reach out to and help others in your circle of friends and acquaintances *before* the trials and difficulties of life overwhelm them. We all need a strong, supportive group of friends.

Jesus Christ came that we all might have life to the full (John 10:10). Let's tell those who are quietly but seriously searching for meaning and purpose about Him—our reason for living! Let's show those who struggle with alienation and loneliness that someone really cares.

TO PONDER

• Have you ever thought of ending your life? Did you talk to a close friend, or keep your struggle to yourself?

• Do you know anyone in your family, circle of acquaintances, or community who attempted to take his or her life? Were there any warning signs before he or she tried to commit suicide?

TO PURSUE

• If you know someone who seems to be losing his or her desire to live (instead of merely to exist)—or if you know someone who may be struggling with the temptation to end his or her life—reach out to that person today with a phone call or visit.

• Pray for boldness to talk to that person about the Lord.

Avoiding the
Elijah Syndrome

A fifty-five-year-old woman threw herself from her four-teen-floor apartment to the ground below. Minutes before her death, she saw a workman washing the windows of a nearby building. She greeted him and smiled, and he smiled and said hello to her. When he turned his back, she jumped.

On a very neat and orderly desk she had left this note: "I can't endure one more day of this loneliness. My phone never rings! I never get letters! I don't have any friends!"

Another woman who lived just across the hall told reporters, "I wish I had known she felt so lonely. I'm lonesome myself."

You and I are surrounded by lonely people.

Who experiences loneliness and despair? The person living anonymously in a crowded city. The foreigner. The rich and miserly. The divorcee and single parent. The young person. The business executive. The unemployed.

No one is immune from loneliness. Even godly men and women sometimes experience loneliness in their pilgrimage through this world.

Elijah stands out in the Old Testament as God's most dramatic, forceful prophet. He stopped the rain, challenged a king face to face, produced fire from heaven, ordered hundreds of false prophets executed, and accurately predicted the day when a three-year drought would end.

Yet in the New Testament we read, "Elijah was a man just like us" (James 5:17). He also experienced times of loneliness and despair.

By taking four wrong steps Elijah found himself under a tree in complete discouragement (1 Kings 18:46–19:4).

First, he exhausted himself physically. Second, he became upset emotionally. Third, he failed to turn to God spiritually. Fourth, he isolated himself socially.

In the end he collapsed under a tree in a desert place and cried, "I've had enough, Lord! Take my life. I just feel like dying."

Have you ever felt completely discouraged—without anyone to encourage you? Have you ever experienced the Elijah syndrome?

Notice how God met each of Elijah's needs in his time of crisis. Physically, God gave him nourishment and sleep. Emotionally, God made His presence known to Elijah and encouraged him. Spiritually, God exhorted Elijah to follow Him once again. Socially, God told Elijah about a large number of godly men and women with whom he could fellowship and receive further encouragement.

God wants to meet your particular needs as well. You cannot live the victorious Christian life alone and on your own; it's impossible. We experience victory only by the power of the indwelling Christ (Galatians 2:20). His presence and power are particularly evident when two or three of His people gather together (Matthew 18:20).

Use your loneliness or discouragement as a motivation to commit yourself anew to the Lord. Don't sit under the tree of despair any longer. Christ has promised to be with us always (Matthew 28:20). He wants to be our best Friend. You never have to feel alone again.

Be sure to fellowship with God's people (Hebrews 10:25), and stop trying to face the daily battles of life by yourself. Pray with others about mutual needs and concerns. Experience God at work in the body of Christ. Victory in the Christian life is a team effort!

TO PONDER

• Have you ever experienced the Elijah syndrome? Did you turn to God? If so, how did He meet you at your point of need?

• Are you actively involved in a local church? Do you belong to a small fellowship group within your church, as well?

TO PURSUE

• In your small group, or when you're together with one or more Christian friends, open up about a personal area of need. Together, pray about that need. And be sure to report back later about how God answers your prayers!

Cultivating a Sexual Counterrevolution

"My husband is overseas," a woman told me. "He has been gone for nine months and will be gone for seven more. I'm lonely and need affection and love. I'm a Christian, but I realize that I am very weak. How can I overcome sexual temptation?"

How would you counsel this woman?

The desire for love and affection reaches deep into the soul. Loneliness also touches the human heart deeply. No one experiences it as acutely as someone who is separated from a spouse because of military service, work, divorce, disability, or death. Sexual desires seem to increase when one's spouse is gone for some length of time.

The Bible speaks clearly concerning sex outside of marriage. But sometimes our sexual desires feel at odds with those Scriptures.

The sexual revolution boldly proclaimed that the biblical imperatives concerning sex only within marriage were outdated and invalid. Proponents of the sexual revolution said that if you were lonely and desired affection, you had a *right* to have those needs met through an illicit affair.

Maybe it is all right to commit immorality in certain circumstances, people rationalized. Trial marriage, group sex, spouse swapping, and other sexual experiments became increasingly popular in certain circles.

But some proponents now regret their efforts to promote the sexual revolution. One of them, George Leonard, admitted, "What I have learned is that there are no games without rules." People can try to break God's moral laws, but they always will have to pay the consequences.

Leonard cited a *Cosmopolitan* survey in which 106,000 women confirmed that a revolution in sexual attitudes and behavior had taken place on both sides of the Atlantic. But how did the women feel about the revolution? Most were disappointed, even disillusioned, with "the emotional fruit the sex revolution has borne." The survey report openly suggested that "there might be a sexual counterrevolution under way."

The Bible clearly warns us not to be deceived, for God will not be mocked. "A man reaps what he sows. The one who sows to please his sinful nature, from that nature will reap destruction" (Galatians 6:7–8).

The destructive harvest of our society's sexual promiscuity—AIDS, herpes, and other venereal diseases; emotional scars; desertion; and spiritual shipwreck—has been a high price to pay for the momentary pleasures of sowing to the flesh.

Scripture says to resist the satanic sexual revolution by committing yourself to God (James 4:7). Confess your sins and draw near to Him. Persevere under temptation by remembering that, as long as we are pilgrims here on earth, God always will provide a way of escape (1 Corinthians 10:13).

Whatever your marital status, God understands your particular temptations and needs. Trust Him to supply "all your needs according to his glorious riches in Christ Jesus" (Philippians 4:19). No matter what everyone else may be doing, take God's eternal Word to heart. In dependence upon God, start your own sexual counterrevolution today.

TO PONDER

• Are you single, married, widowed, separated, or divorced? Are you sexually active? To what degree are you tempted sexually? How are you dealing with such temptation?

TO PURSUE

• Honestly confess any sexual immorality to the Lord, humbly asking for His forgiveness and cleansing. Ask Him to keep you pure in an impure world.

Learning About Love, Marriage, and Sex

I was only twelve, but I felt like a man. School was out for the summer, and I was helping with the family business. The work was a refreshing break from my just-completed exams.

This particular day I was helping deliver a load of cement bags. The driver, a twenty-year-old laborer, seemed friendly and boosted my ego as we worked together.

"Luis," he said as we pulled over to the side of the road, "since you are becoming a young man now and you have no father, you need someone to talk to you about the facts of life."

My heart began to pound. I was excited to think I might get some straight answers from someone who really knew the score.

But instead of telling me anything, the truck driver simply opened a magazine and turned the pages while I stared in unbelief at the pictures of naked men and women. I was shocked and disgusted.

Later, I could not push the images from my mind. I felt sinful, degraded, horrible, guilty. Impure thoughts invaded my mind. I had been curious before, but had always resisted the temptation to look at such magazines. Now one was thrown at me unexpectedly, and I was repulsed.

It wasn't until I was twenty-three that a man talked to me plainly from the Bible about human sexuality. I was amazed by how much the Bible actually says about sex.

I think it's a crime that, as God's pilgrims journeying through this world, we leave sex education to other people and institutions that usually teach only about the physical aspects of reproduction and anatomy. We need to understand and teach what God says about the total spectrum of love, marriage, and sex.

1. *The Bible teaches that God created sex.* God made Adam and Eve as perfect, sexual beings (Genesis 2:18–25). Not until after the fall of humankind did Satan tempt people to misuse and abuse this gift.

Often adults communicate to their children by their stubborn silence that sex is somehow evil. That's false! Sex, in my opinion, is one of the most beautiful gifts God has given humanity.

2. *The Bible shows that God created sex for pleasure as well as for reproduction.* God's Word exalts the joys of marital love. See the Song of Solomon, for example. Scripture likewise speaks of children as a special blessing from the Lord (Psalm 127:3).

3. *The Bible presents sex as wholesome and right only within marriage.* Hebrews 13:4 says, "Marriage should be honored by all, and the marriage bed kept pure, for God will judge the adulterer and all the sexually immoral."

Only six percent of the young adults questioned for a survey indicated that by age twenty-one they were still waiting for God's ideal—sexual intimacy only in marriage. God's beautiful gift has been distorted and cheapened in so many cases.

How were your own views of love, marriage, and sex formed? Are they consistent with what the Bible teaches? In an age of confused immorality, we need to personally study and understand what God says about wholesome sexuality.

TO PONDER

• Do you feel you have a clear, biblical understanding of sex now? To what degree?

• Think back to how you learned about sexuality. Did you have any experiences that left you feeling defiled? If so, what did you do about it?

TO PURSUE

• In John 13, Jesus washed His disciples feet, cleansing them from the defilement of the world. Ask the Lord to cleanse you from any defilement you've experienced.

Avoiding a Midlife Crisis

Scripture always strikes me as true to life. It never glosses over unpleasant facts. The Bible helps each of us understand and deal with our problems because it frankly discusses the problems of those who have gone on before us.

King David, for example, started out well for the Lord. He zealously served God as a young man. Even when he had to run for his life month after month, he remained true to God's commandments.

But as David reached middle age, he encountered three perils that caught him off guard (2 Samuel 11). Each of us will also face these same perils at some point in our pilgrimage through this world. If we fail to respond properly to these perils, we will experience what psychologists call a "midlife crisis."

What are these perils? The first is *the peril of growing weary.* David experienced this weariness after years of fighting against the enemies of Israel. Instead of attacking the Ammonites with his army, as he should have, David decided to stay home one spring and relax in Jerusalem (2 Samuel 11:1).

Weariness hits when you've been out in the working world some ten, fifteen, or twenty years. Maybe you've been married for just as long. Life becomes routine, and weariness easily convinces us at this point to take it easy for a change.

Second, with weariness comes *the peril of carelessness.* No one wakes up Monday morning and says, "Hey, I think I'll wreck my marriage today." But how often we hear of Christian couples who separate after ten or twenty years of marriage. Why? Because they were careless.

Third, with carelessness comes *the peril of confusion.* David failed to follow the spiritual compass of God's Word and the guiding of the Holy Spirit. He inquired about a certain woman, and before the night was over he committed adultery (2 Samuel 11:3–4).

When you are young, you know just where you want to be when you reach forty. Then you get there and feel trapped by your responsibilities, your job, and your marriage. What do you do when Satan offers you a tantalizing change of pace? How should you respond to the perils of middle age?

Take a few moments and read 2 Timothy. It's a very short letter. In this epistle the apostle Paul explains how to avoid a midlife crisis. "Timothy," Paul says, "don't give up. Persist. Shun youthful lusts. Be steady. Continue in the things you have learned. Fulfill your ministry."

As you read 2 Timothy, write down all the ways to resist Satan's temptations to relax and become careless spiritually. Also observe the images Paul uses to describe this steadfastness—a single-minded soldier, a disciplined athlete, a hard-working farmer, a faithful workman, a persistent fighter, a never-say-quit runner.

When you face the perils of weariness, carelessness, and confusion—whether or not you are middle-aged—don't pray for an easier life. Pray instead to be a stronger man or woman of God.

TO PONDER

• How old are you? Have you experienced any of the perils of midlife? Do you feel more weary, or careless, or confused at this point in your life?

TO PURSUE

• As suggested above, take a few minutes to read 2 Timothy. Underline or highlight all the passages speaking about staying true to the Lord despite the perils of midlife.

Wrestling with
Unemployment

Who do you know who is out of work? Someone in your family? A friend? Perhaps even you have wrestled with unemployment recently.

I wrestled with unemployment while supporting my widowed mother and five younger sisters in Argentina. In those days massive strikes shook my home country. I was without work, without relief, without anything!

Whenever unemployment strikes, it creates unique marital, financial, and even medical problems. It also prematurely exposes a person to the perils usually associated with middle age: *weariness, carelessness,* and *confusion.* These very terms describe many of the unemployed today.

What should a committed Christian do if he finds himself out of work? I believe the Bible gives us several specific principles that relate to the issue of unemployment.

First, accept your unemployment, even though it may be difficult, and trust God to use it for good. The Bible tells us that "in all things God works for the good of those who love him, who have been called according to his purpose" (Romans 8:28).

Second, carefully plan how to use your extra time in the best way possible. In Ephesians 5:15–16 we read, "Be very careful, then, how you live—not as unwise but as wise, making the most of every opportunity."

If you are unemployed, I suggest that you spend the first two hours of every day in Bible study and prayer. Spend the next three or four hours looking seriously and systematically for a job.

Third, minister to other people during your spare time. Organize a Bible study with others who are unemployed, and pray together. Spend time discipling new believers.

As an individual or a group, use your afternoons to work for your church, help those in need, visit the elderly, or actively evangelize in your community.

God's Word says, "Let us not become weary in doing good, for at the proper time we will reap a harvest if we do not give up" (Galatians 6:9). I believe God will compensate those who volunteer to help others, if they do it for His glory.

Fourth, be a good steward of your time, energy, and possessions. Work together as a family to see how you can creatively use what you already possess to meet some of your needs, and even help others.

Perhaps you have some land. Plant a garden! Perhaps you have certain talents that could be used to earn some money. Use them!

In Matthew 6:33 we read, "Seek first his kingdom and his righteousness, and all these things will be given to you as well." As we honor God in every part of our lives, we can be sure He will supply everything we need.

If unemployment strikes your home, I challenge you to seek God's kingdom and righteousness. Act on the principles outlined above and trust God to provide your every need.

TO PONDER

• Have you ever experienced unemployment? When and for how long? Was it a time of spiritual struggle, growth, or both?

TO PURSUE

• Do you have a Christian friend who is currently unemployed? If so, invite that friend (and his or her family) over for a meal. Don't feel you have to tell him or her all the principles I've outlined above. But do listen to how your friend is doing and offer practical assistance, as you are able.

Dealing with Sin

Billy Staton slipped a tape recorder into his shirt pocket before going to pick up his daughter for a picnic, planning to tape his ex-wife's hostility about his visitation rights.

Instead, Staton recorded his own slaying in what one prosecutor called "twenty-three minutes of murder." Paul Wolf, twenty-one, was charged with Staton's murder. The tape conclusively revealed that Wolf committed the murder. But he pleaded *innocent* to the slaying!

Wolf's attorney explained to the jurors that his client was innocent because he was "legally insane" on the day of the killing. He explained that Wolf had suffered a difficult childhood with a mentally ill mother and a hard-driving father, then faced an ongoing series of custody problems after his marriage to Staton's ex-wife.

The attorney explained that Wolf did not plan the killing, but was *forced* to slay Staton "at the last minute after the steady, lengthy, continual buildup of the pressure."

Such lawyers fill our court records day after day with excuses for their clients' actions. But no matter what the courts decide, such men and women must live with their heavy burden of guilt.

In our society, some lawyers and psychologists have tried to replace personal responsibility and sin with scientific-sounding explanations for wrongdoing.

Whatever happened to sin?

O. Hobart Mowrer, a noted psychologist, stated: "For several decades we psychologists looked upon the whole matter of sin and moral accountability as a great incubus, and acclaimed our liberation from it as epoch making. But at length we have discovered that to be 'free' in this sense, that is to have the excuse of being 'sick' rather than sinful, is to court the danger of also being lost."

Another noted psychologist, Rex Julian Beaber, said this: "The force of evil has disappeared from nature; sinfulness is no longer man's fate. The new 'sciences' of sociology, psychology and psychiatry have cast aside such concepts as will, will power, badness, and laziness, and replaced them with political and psychological repression, poor conditioning, diseased family interaction, and bad genes. One by one, human failings have been redesignated as diseases."

Beaber counters this modern trend by stating, "Ultimately, we *must* assume responsibility for our actions." Sin must be rediscovered once more in our generation.

If you scratch under the surface, most people carry burdens of guilt nobody else knows about. We hide this guilt as a skeleton in the closet of our souls. At the advice of our psychiatrists, we deny its existence. We explain it away. We repress it. We do anything but admit our failure. Ironically, until we make such an admission, our closet full of guilt will continue to haunt us.

Rudyard Kipling said it well: "Nothing is ever settled until it is settled right." We can point the finger and make up excuses, we can invent arguments and do anything else we want to do, but the key to the closet jingles in our pockets until we settle matters right.

Proverbs 28:13 says, "He who conceals his sins does not prosper, but whoever confesses and renounces them finds mercy." In a day of permissive dropout, cop-out, rip-off, and let-yourself-go, we need to learn the foundational principle of all mental, social, and spiritual health. We need to learn to confess and forsake our *sins* in order to experience forgiveness.

TO PONDER

• Why do we so often want to cover up or excuse our sins, instead of owning up to them? What happens as a result?

TO PURSUE

• Privately, ask God to reveal any unconfessed and unforsaken sin in your life.

PART THREE

Practicing Obedience
as God's Servant

*Although formerly we walked in the ways of
the world, the Lord Jesus now calls us to walk
as His servants, in holiness of life.*

■ *Habit*

Avoiding Spiritual Banana Peels

Only four chapters in the Bible remain silent about sin and its dangers—the first two and the last two. Since Adam and Eve found themselves naked under the tree of the knowledge of good and evil, sin has been the lowest common denominator throughout the human race.

The apostle John spells this out clearly: "If we claim to be without sin, we deceive ourselves and the truth is not in us" (1 John 1:8). The deadliest sin is assuming we have no sin. None of us is free from the possibility of committing evil. Until we enjoy fruit from the tree of life in glory someday, we must admit our vulnerability.

"If you're saying some sin could never get you," Dr. Howard Hendricks writes, "you're about to step on a spiritual banana peel."

You and I both know of Christian leaders and lay people who have "suddenly" fallen into sin. Everything seemed to be going well for them, but one left his wife for another woman, or one attempted suicide, or one became an alcoholic.

How does this happen? Dr. George Sweeting comments, "Collapse in the Christian life is rarely a blowout—it's usually a slow leak."

Our spiritual lives are punctured and in danger of collapse whenever we lose sight of who God is. To the degree that we do not know God, we sin. Sin is man's declaration of independence. The first step away from God is ceasing to appreciate who God is and failing to thank Him for His person and work in our lives.

Unthankfulness and other forms of disobedience—whether in deed, thought, or desire—produce certain results. When we sin the Holy Spirit is grieved, Satan gains a foothold, we lose our joy in Christ, we find ourselves separated from God and other people, we become stumbling blocks to weaker believers, and we cause untold sorrow and grief.

Take spiritual inventory in your own life. Consider: *Who is God in my eyes? What is my relationship with Him like? How often do I give thanks to Him?* Meditate on such passages as Psalm 34, Psalm 63:1–8, and 1 Thessalonians 5:16–24. Determine ways to apply these passages to your own life.

What comes to mind when you think about God is the most important thing about you. What comes from your lips throughout the day indicates whether or not you see and appreciate His sovereignty, His grace, and the other attributes of His deity.

Is the Lord speaking to your heart? How is your relationship with Him? Confess any known sins to God, and decide that by God's enabling you will live a life of holiness. Speak forth the praises of the Lord you love, and faithfully obey Him.

Collapse in the Christian life never needs to happen!

TO PONDER

• When are you and I most in danger of stepping on a spiritual banana peel?
• When we sin, what happens?

TO PURSUE

• Quietly confess any known sin to the Lord. Thank Him for His forgiveness.

Experiencing
God's Forgiveness

During World War II Hans Rookmaaker became active in the Dutch Resistance. Eventually he was captured by the Germans and sent to a Nazi concentration camp, where he began to read the Bible.

As he studied God's Word, he discovered for himself that at the heart of God is the desire to forgive our sins. He gladly committed his life to Christ and reveled in his new-found joy and freedom to please and serve the Lord.

When Rookmaaker was released from prison at the end of the war, he immediately joined a church. But instead of fellowshiping with the free, he was surprised to find many Christians still in bondage to sin. They were not experiencing God's forgiveness.

On the other hand, a character in a play by Voltaire died muttering, "God will forgive—that's His job." Forgiveness cannot be presupposed like that, but God never meant for us to live in bondage to sin, either.

The Bible teaches that confession is prerequisite to God's forgiveness, whether for initial salvation or daily fellowship. This confession involves repentance and, when necessary, restitution.

Confession without repentance constitutes fraud. In Proverbs 28:13 we read, "He who conceals his sins does not prosper, but whoever confesses and renounces them finds mercy."

Confession sometimes involves restitution (Exodus 22:1–15). Usually this is the forgotten aspect of confession. But if our sin deprived someone of something that was rightfully his (whether goods or money or an honest amount of work), we must not only apologize to the offended person but also seek to repay him as soon as possible.

The beauty of Scripture is its good news that God freely forgives those who properly confess their sins. Manasseh was one of the most wicked men to serve as king of Judah. He overturned Hezekiah's reforms and served false gods with more zeal than the nations whom God had destroyed (2 Chronicles 33:1–9). But after being captured by the Assyrians, Manasseh greatly humbled himself before the Lord—and God forgave him!

If God could forgive such a wicked king who humbled himself, surely He will forgive us when we truly confess our sins and repent. Confession is humbling, but "if we confess our sins, he is faithful and just and will forgive us our sins and purify us from all unrighteousness" (1 John 1:9). Learn this verse and claim it—often.

Here is another good verse to add to your Scripture memorization list: "Their sins and lawless acts I will remember no more" (Hebrews 10:17). How remarkable it is that the omniscient God promises not only to forgive our sins, but also to forget them forever!

TO PONDER

• Why is it so hard to make things right with others? Why is it so liberating?

TO PURSUE

• Make a list of those whom you need to ask for forgiveness and make restitution. By each name, write a date when you will visit that person to make things right.

Recognizing
Perpetual Commotion

During the seventeenth century the Marquis of Worchester found himself imprisoned in the Tower of London. Being a clever gentleman, he built a curious contraption and asked for an audience with the king.

In the king's presence he revealed his invention: a self-turning wheel. His majesty was so impressed he released his prisoner. Little did he suspect at the time that the marquis had simply *simulated* a perpetual motion machine.

For at least 1,500 years various individuals have tried to design and build the world's first unpowered device that never stops moving. During the golden age of perpetual motion in England, from about 1850 to the turn of the century, nearly 600 patents for such devices were granted. The contraptions certainly look impressive on paper, but when built they never work!

Contemporary perpetual motionists refuse to concede that it is impossible to break the laws of thermodynamics. Their "perpetual commotion" only succeeds in redesigning machines that were proven failures generations ago.

Similarly, men and women today ignore the clear statements of Scripture in their attempts to achieve the impossible. Futilely they seek to obtain eternal life and favor with God by their good deeds. Salvation, however, is not granted on the merits of our attainment, but on Christ's perfect atonement for our sins by His death on the cross. Only by committing our lives to Him can we receive the assurance of sins forgiven and life eternal.

Salvation by works is a type of perpetual commotion. It will never work. In Romans 3:23 we read, "All have sinned and fall short of the glory of God." No matter how hard we try, we can't measure up to the perfect standard God requires before anyone can enter His presence. Salvation can never be achieved on the basis of what we do, but only on the basis of God's infinite mercy.

A mother once approached Napoleon seeking a pardon for her son. The emperor replied that the young man had committed a certain offense twice, and justice demanded death.

"But I don't ask for justice," the mother explained. "I plead for mercy."

"But your son does not deserve mercy," Napoleon replied.

"Sir," the woman cried, "it would not be mercy if he deserved it, and mercy is all I ask for."

"Well, then," the emperor said, "I will have mercy." And he spared the woman's son.

Christians are not those who earn God's favor by their intrinsic goodness; they are merely recipients of God's mercy. God saves us, we read in Titus 3:5, not because of the righteous things we have done, but because of His mercy. Thankfully, we need ask but once in order to receive His gift of salvation freely.

Just as salvation is not *attained* by what we do, so it is not *maintained* by our good works as God's servants. Our salvation rests on the sure promises of God. Christ Himself has gone on record as saying, "I tell you the truth, whoever hears my word and believes him who sent me has eternal life and will not be condemned; he has crossed over from death to life" (John 5:24).

All the perpetual commotion in the world cannot save an individual no matter how ingenious his or her efforts may appear. And all the uproar in hell cannot change the certainty of God's salvation once we receive it.

TO PONDER

• On what are you depending for salvation?

• Are you saved because you're God's servant, or are you God's servant because you're saved?

TO PURSUE

• Stand up if you're alone. Lift your hands to the Lord and thank Him for your salvation. Then kneel and commit yourself to God as His obedient servant.

Letting Go of Guilt

As Christians we rejoice that our salvation is secure in Christ, and that our sins are forever washed away by His blood. We marvel at God's infinite mercy to forgive us even though we don't deserve it. But often we won't forgive ourselves!

Yes, we know that "as far as the east is from the west, so far has he removed our transgressions from us" (Psalm 103:12). But from sunrise to sunset we needlessly carry the heavy burden of guilt.

For some reason we feel compelled to carry these heavy burdens, even though God never asked us to carry them. Just the opposite! So as God's servants, we need to learn to let go of our guilt.

Sometimes our burden of guilt is nothing more than false condemnation. When I was a youth, my mother absolutely believed the bottom of the theater would open up and drop me straight into the fire of hell if I ever went to see a movie, regardless of its message. I felt bad even walking by a theater. Now *that* was false guilt!

Paul Tournier, a respected Swiss psychologist, has said, "False guilt comes as a result of judgments and suggestions of men." People sometimes seek to control or manipulate us by inventing rules or regulations the Bible never mentions. As servants of God, not slaves to man-made decrees, we need to carefully and prayerfully identify such false guilt and let go of it.

On other occasions we carry heavy burdens of guilt because we don't deal with it properly. There are at least three inappropriate responses to true guilt.

First, we can *repress* our guilt. We try to cover it up and deny its existence. We focus on our insignificant faults instead of acknowledging our real guilt. As a result, we lose our peace and often suffer physically as well.

Second, we can *regret* our "mistake." But merely saying "I'm sorry" fails to acknowledge the seriousness of our sin and our responsibility.

Third, we can feel *remorse* for our sin. "I'll never do it again," we promise. Judas felt remorse after betraying Christ (Matthew 27:3–4). But he fell one step short of what the Bible calls repentance.

Repentance is the biblical, correct response to guilt. The moment we committed our life to Christ, our sins—past, present, and future—were forgiven. God's righteousness was satisfied. But now we must maintain fellowship with, dependence on, and obedience to God. This necessitates confessing our sins to our Lord as we become aware of them.

C.S. Lewis said true guilt is an inner alarm system that reveals sin in our lives and shows our loss of fellowship with God. The Holy Spirit uses guilt to prompt us to turn *from* our sin and back *to* the Lord.

Once we let go of false guilt and properly deal with our sins, we are free from the burden of guilt. Isaiah 55:6–7 gives us this assurance: "Seek the Lord while he may be found; call on him while he is near. Let the wicked forsake his way and the evil man his thoughts. Let him turn to the Lord, and he will have mercy on him, and to our God, for he will freely pardon."

Let go of your burdens and turn to God today!

TO PONDER

• Is there any unresolved guilt in your life? Over what? What steps, if any, have you taken so far to try to resolve it?

• In Matthew 11:29–30, Jesus promises His burdens are not heavy. It doesn't make sense, then, to carry a load of guilt. Why not?

TO PURSUE

• If you're struggling with a vague sense of guilt, turn that over to the Lord.

• Ask God to pinpoint any specific, unconfessed sin in your life. As He does, repent of that sin, remembering God gladly forgives and forgets.

Forgiving and Forgetting

Has anyone ever offended you? Has your spouse been unfaithful to you? Have your children disappointed you? Has someone cheated you in business? How we respond to the difficult experiences of life directly affects our spiritual well-being.

My father died when I was only ten years old. He left us quite a bit of property and some money. But several of his brothers squandered everything we had. In three years my family was living in poverty and debt.

When I was older and really understood what my uncles had done, I urged my mother to take revenge on them, to get a lawyer to take them to court and let them have it. The older I got, the more bitter I became.

But the Bible says, "Do not take revenge, my friends, but leave room for God's wrath, for it is written: 'It is mine to avenge; I will repay,' says the Lord" (Romans 12:19). He is the One who measures out justice. He wants to handle such judgments for us—perhaps now, certainly ultimately.

My mother always quoted verses like Romans 12:19. She completely forgave my uncles for what they did. It took us twenty years to finish paying our debts, but she refused to become bitter; she forgot what they had done. Consequently, God gave her a freedom of spirit and special opportunities to serve Him. I experienced that same freedom and fruitfulness years later when I, too, finally forgave my uncles.

How deeply have you been hurt? Have you become bitter or unforgiving in your attitude?

I would like to remind you of the story of Joseph. I encourage you to read the account of his life in Genesis 37–50. It is an exciting portion of Scripture! This passage shows us many valuable lessons on the importance of forgiving and forgetting.

The Bible gives us several reasons why Joseph could have been a very bitter man. His brothers hated him and sold him into slavery. His master's wife falsely accused him of a serious crime and had him thrown into an Egyptian prison. A government official promised to help him but instead left him in prison to rot. Despite all these things, Joseph did not allow any root of bitterness to take hold in his life (Hebrews 12:15).

Many lives are spoiled by bitterness and a lack of forgiveness. People go through physical and emotional breakdowns because they refuse to forgive other people. The longer we carry a grudge, the heavier it becomes. As God's servants, we cannot afford to harbor bitterness in our souls, for it will destroy us.

The Bible says, "Bear with each other and forgive whatever grievances you may have against one another. Forgive as the Lord forgave you" (Colossians 3:13).

After entering into the experience of forgiving someone, forgetfulness is vital. Joseph named his firstborn son Manasseh because "God has made me forget all my trouble and all my father's household" (Genesis 41:51). Joseph not only forgave his brothers, but also forgot the evil deeds they had committed against him.

Like Joseph, keep short accounts with God and people. Don't lock bitterness and guilt within the closet of your soul. Forgive and forget. This is an essential habit for spiritual health and growth.

TO PONDER

• If you refuse to forgive and forget the offenses of others, who suffers the consequences?

• In Matthew 6:14–15, Jesus teaches that your relationship with God is directly affected every time you choose whether or not to forgive someone else. In what way?

TO PURSUE

• Take five minutes to begin reading the story of Joseph in Genesis 37. Later this week, take time to read the rest of this fast-paced narrative. As you read, consciously think of those who have hurt you and, in prayer, ask for God's enabling to forgive them and forget their offenses.

Doing What
Our Father Says

More than ninety people conducted an all-night search for Dominic DeCarlo, an eight-year-old boy lost on a snowy mountain slope. Dominic, who had been on a skiing trip with his father, apparently had ridden on a new lift and skied off the run without realizing it.

As each hour passed, the search party and the boy's family became more and more concerned for his health and safety. By dawn they had found no trace of the boy. Two helicopter crews joined the search, and within fifteen minutes they spotted ski tracks. A ground team followed the tracks, which changed to small footprints. The footprints led to a tree, where they found the boy at last.

"He's in super shape!" Sergeant Terry Silbaugh, area search-and-rescue coordinator, announced to the anxious family and press. "In fact, he's in better shape than we are right now!" A hospital spokeswoman said the boy was in fine condition, so he wasn't even admitted.

Silbaugh explained why the boy did so well despite spending a night in the freezing elements: His father had enough forethought to warn the boy what to do if he became lost, and his son had enough trust to do exactly what his father said.

Dominic protected himself from possible frostbite and hypothermia by snuggling up to a tree and covering himself with branches. As a young child, he never would have thought of doing this on his own. He was simply obeying his wise and loving father.

Dominic reminds me of what we should do as servants, as pilgrims, and as children of our loving and infinitely wise heavenly Father. We are not to walk according to the course of this world, which is passing away. Instead, we are to walk in obedience to the Lord's commands. After all, He knows what is best for us. That's one of the reasons I believe the Bible is so relevant for us today.

The apostle Peter tells us, "As obedient children, do not conform to the evil desires you had when you lived in ignorance. But just as he who called you is holy, so be holy in all you do; for it is written: 'Be holy, because I am holy' " (1 Peter 1:14–16).

In Christ we enjoy a holy *standing* before God. In 2 Corinthians 5:21 we discover that "God made him who had no sin to be sin for us, so that in him we might become the righteousness of God." But our actual *state* here on earth is sometimes a different story.

Because our Father is holy, and because in Christ we have a holy standing, we are exhorted in Scripture to be holy in all that we do. Every time we sin, we are forgetting who we are and why we are alive. We are forgetting what is truly best for us. Yes, we can find forgiveness from the Father when we sin (1 John 2:1–2), but sin is not to be the trademark of our lives.

In a world full of deceptive detours and confusing paths, let's trust our Father and do exactly what He says.

TO PONDER

- Do you believe God knows what is best for you? If you're hesitant to answer an emphatic "yes," why?

- What is the trademark of your life? What trademark do you want from now on?

TO PURSUE

- On a 3"x5" card, write out 1 Peter 1:14–16. Read these verses over a few times. During the next week, memorize these key verses and meditate on them. Then put them into practice!

God's Fences
for Freedom

Do God's commandments excite you? Do you enjoy studying them—and obeying them? When was the last time, for example, you seriously contemplated the Ten Commandments?

When I was growing up in Argentina, God's commandments—especially the Ten Commandments—were taught in such a legalistic way that I avoided any serious study of them until after I had finished my graduate level biblical studies in the United States. I discovered then how little has ever been written about them.

Our sinful nature causes us to corrupt that which is beautiful. We turn God's moral law, which the apostle Paul called "holy, righteous and good" (Romans 7:12), into oppressive legalism. Perhaps that's why we frown at the mere mention of the Ten Commandments.

"They remind me of my grandmother, who had a fit if I ever wanted to play outside on Sundays," some will admit.

"Thinking of the commandments reminds me of my father, who refused to read the Sunday newspaper."

The words of God should not elicit such reactions. Let's return to God's moral law and shake off the chains of sincere but sinful human beings who have twisted the beauty of God's commandments.

When the Lord gave Israel the Ten Commandments, He said, "Listen, O Israel! I brought you out of bondage, not to create another bondage for you, but to liberate you. And if you remain within the boundaries I am about to give you, then you will be free. You'll have plenty of room to maneuver. So enjoy all that I have given you."

God's statement includes a warning: "As long as you stay within the fence, you will be free, but once you try to stretch the boundaries or jump over the fence, you will be in bondage once again."

I am convinced this is the way God intends us to view His commandments. The apostle John reminds us, "His commands are not burdensome" (1 John 5:3). They are life!

Now obviously we are not to try to live up to the Ten Commandments for our salvation. We are all sinners (Romans 3:23) in need of a Savior, Jesus Christ (Romans 5:8). Both the Bible and experience teach us we couldn't keep the Ten Commandments perfectly even if we tried (Romans 7:1–8:4).

The purpose of God's commandments is not to provide salvation but to lay a foundation for us—a foundation on which to build a life of love and obedience as God's servants.

Spend some time meditating on God's commandments. Start with the Ten Commandments in Exodus 20:1–17. As you study and pray, answer these questions. First, what does each commandment reveal about the character of God? Second, what does each commandment liberate me from? Third, how does each commandment protect me? Finally, if love is the fulfillment of the law (Galatians 5:14), then what does each of the commandments reveal about love?

I believe once you answer these four questions, you will never look at God's commandments with a negative attitude again. As you look at them with a new perspective, I think you will uncover at least four principles that will enhance your understanding of our infinitely wise and loving heavenly Father.

TO PONDER

• Count how many of the Ten Commandments you can remember by heart. Three? Five? How many?

• When you've thought about the Ten Commandments in the past, what has been your reaction? What is your reaction now?

TO PURSUE

• Take out your Bible, a pen, and paper. Take a few minutes to study Exodus 20:1–17, answering the four questions listed above. Then proceed to Habit 34.

Meeting God
Within His Fences

In the last habit, we considered how people often turn God's commandments into oppressive legalism when God meant them to liberate us!

In my personal study of the Ten Commandments, I have learned four principles that have enhanced my understanding of our heavenly Father's infinite wisdom and love.

1. *God's commandments reveal His character.* To me, the most exciting aspect of the Ten Commandments is what they reveal about God's character. See how the list from your study for the last habit compares with mine.

We worship a God who is possessive (Exodus 20:3); who is jealous, in that He hates idolatry (20:4–6); who is holy and honorable, deserving of respect (20:7); who wants us to preserve the sanctity of worship and learn to rest in Him (20:8–11); who wants to protect the family (20:12); who reveres life (20:13); who desires godly offspring, sexual purity, and holy people (20:14); who delights in giving gifts and not having them taken away (20:15); who can be trusted one hundred percent (20:16); who looks on the inner reality of each heart (20:17).

How do our lists compare? Aren't the Ten Commandments a great place to start a study on holiness and the character of God?

2. *God's commandments provide genuine liberation.* Today's society generates a tremendous sense of bondage. People constantly talk about their need to break away, to go out on their own and be free. People believe breaking God's moral law is the road to liberation. Ironically, all they experience is further enslavement. Only God's moral laws provide genuine liberation. This seems especially true in dating and marital relationships.

3. *God's commandments provide complete protection.* After reading the Ten Commandments carefully, can you see how God designed them to protect us socially, politically, economically, and physically? And most of all, do you see how they protect us spiritually from our adversary, the devil, who would like nothing better than to destroy us? (1 Peter 5:8).

One of the ways Satan battles us is by tempting us to climb over one of God's fences. But, as God's servants, we can have victory because Christ indwells us (1 John 4:4).

4. *God's commandments reveal true love.* Did you read through the Ten Commandments to learn what each command reveals about love? Let's compare lists again.

I reveal *my love* for the Father by giving Him His unique and proper supreme place in my life (Exodus 20:3); by not attributing characteristics to Him that are not revealed in Scripture (20:4–6); by not grieving the Holy Spirit with an undisciplined tongue (20:7); by setting aside a day each week for honoring God and fellowshiping with my family and the family of God (20:8–11); by honoring my parents, which ultimately reveals God's love toward us in our older years and His desire that we have happy homes (20:12); by respecting life and doing to others as we would have them do to us (20:13); by not playing games with our sexuality (20:14); by delighting in being generous for the Lord (20:15); by being trustworthy and God-honoring in our speech (20:16); by being content, holy, and sanctified through the power of the Holy Spirit who dwells in us (20:17).

God's commandments also reveal *His vast love* for us. Because we could never measure up to His glory and holiness, He provided us with a Savior—His Son, Jesus Christ. When we repent, seek forgiveness, and commit ourselves to Christ, He comes to live in us. It is only then, by His power, that we can live in obedience to Him and experience His blessing in our lives.

TO PONDER

• To you, what is the most exciting aspect of God's Ten Commandments?

• In a Bible study discussion, someone makes a disparaging comment about the Ten Commandments and then asks how you feel about God's commandments. How would you respond?

TO PURSUE

• In the margin of your Bible, on the page for Exodus 20:1–17, write: "God's commandments reveal His character and love, and provide both liberation and protection."

Out-of-Bounds

The boundary line seemed old and irrelevant. Sarah tapped the line with her foot, wondering what would happen if she crossed it. At last, at the persuasion of her boyfriend, Andy, she stepped over the line.

Several weeks later, sixteen-year-old Sarah discovered she was pregnant. "I'll never forget the panic," she admits. "Andy was in Cyprus, and I was living at home with my Dad. . . . I just didn't know where to turn."

Andy came back from overseas and the two teenagers were married. But Sarah's problems are far from solved. Loneliness, financial pressures, and regret plague her.

"I hope Andy and I will stay together, though being a soldier he's away a lot, and I get bored being stuck at home all day," Sarah confesses. "So maybe one day we'll split up. The thing is, you have to try so hard to make marriage work, and divorce is so easy."

God's standard of sexual purity before marriage seemed out-of-date to Sarah. She didn't realize God had wisely and lovingly established that boundary for her own protection. Now she is suffering the consequences of her disobedience.

What are the consequences of going out-of-bounds sexually, whether single or married? Ask King David. In Psalm 38 he describes the effects of his personal sin—perhaps that of committing adultery with Bathsheba.

David experienced the agony of spiritual discipline (verses 1–2), physical torment (verses 3–10), social isolation (verses 11–16), and emotional anxiety (verses 17–22). Quite a high price to pay for a moment of uncontrolled passion, wouldn't you say?

God's standards for purity in interpersonal relationships are far from out-of-date, even though they contradict today's cultural norms.

Youth today say that premarital sex is okay. One poll indicates ninety-four percent forfeit their virginity by age twenty-one. But God says: "Flee from sexual immorality. All other sins a man commits are outside his body, but he who sins sexually sins against his own body. Do you not know that your body is a temple of the Holy Spirit, who is in you, whom you have received from God? You are not your own; you were bought at a price. Therefore honor God with your body" (1 Corinthians 6:18–20).

Christian young people struggle with the same temptations their unbelieving peers face. The devil often uses an unhealthy Christian/non-Christian dating relationship to cause a believer to stumble. The Lord warns us: "Do not be yoked together with unbelievers. For what do righteousness and wickedness have in common? Or what fellowship can light have with darkness? What harmony is there between Christ and Belial? What does a believer have in common with an unbeliever? What agreement is there between the temple of God and idols? For we are the temple of the living God" (2 Corinthians 6:14–16).

Especially if you're single, take these verses to heart. As God's servant, committed to practicing obedience in every area of life, develop biblical convictions for dating and relating to persons of the opposite sex. Then enjoy the satisfaction that comes from a Christ-centered relationship kept within His wise and loving boundaries.

TO PONDER

• Why do God's commandments seem so at odds with the standards of the world around us?

• What should you remember and what should you do, as God's servant, when your feelings are at odds with God's commandments about sexual purity?

TO PURSUE

• Take out a sheet of paper and pen. If you have children who aren't married yet, begin making a list of the biblical standards you want them to follow for dating, courtship, and marriage.

• If you're single, write out your own list of standards for dating, courtship, and marriage.

HABIT 36

Dating and Courtship

On the way to a class party one day, I noticed several girls. "Are you going to the party?" I asked. They all said yes, and for some reason I asked one of them, "Can I walk you over?"

She said, "Sure." It was no big deal. We weren't even together at the party, but I started becoming interested in this young woman. Pat was fun and talkative. She seemed mature and intelligent, she knew how to dress well, and in conversation I discovered she was spiritually sensitive.

I don't know what Pat thought of me at first—she still won't tell me—but I began looking for her on campus. In fact, my window overlooked a walkway to the cafeteria, and I watched for her every morning and then "just happened" to pop out the door when she came by.

I had never studied much in the library before, but when I found out Pat usually did her homework there, that's where I could be found too. I kept one eye on my book and the other on her. Pat finally caught on that I was interested in her, and we saw a lot of each other. At first there was nothing serious between us, but I certainly hoped there would be!

I'll be the first to admit I made mistakes while I dated and courted Pat. But let me share some key words with you from my experience that will help you (or your unmarried children) to develop a quality relationship with someone of the opposite sex.

The first word is *courtesy*. Courtesy is a sign of genuine love. By love I don't mean matrimonial love, but the type of love that comes from God. In 1 Corinthians 13:5 we read that love is not rude or self-seeking. Instead, love gives to the other person without planning to get something else in return.

Someone has said, "Good habits are made of little sacrifices." I like that. The habit of courtesy consists of little and insignificant sacrifices that show our interest in the other person. Discover what your special friend enjoys. Does she like flowers? Surprise her with a small bouquet of her favorite. Show thoughtfulness and respect as you spend time together getting to know each other.

Another important word to remember is *conversation*. Paul tells us in Colossians 4:6, "Let your conversation be always full of grace." Nothing is better for a good friendship than positive and uplifting talks. I still remember the many discussions Pat and I enjoyed the year before we were married.

Often relationships between a man and a woman focus—even depend—on showing physical affection. But as Solomon wrote, there is a time to embrace, and a time to refrain (Ecclesiastes 3:5). As God's servants, focus instead on learning more about each other's interests, families, friends, dreams, priorities, and walk with the Lord. Ask lots of questions—*and listen*! The best conversation is the one you initiate with questions.

If you are dating or engaged, talk with your special friend about making courtesy and conversation part of your relationship. In the next habit, I want to share two more key words with you about dating and courtship.

TO PONDER

• If you're married, how would you characterize the period you dated and courted the person who is now your spouse? What lessons could others learn from your experience?

• If you're single, what lessons can you learn from the experience of others?

TO PURSUE

• Review the two principles discussed above, then proceed to Habit 37.

More About
Dating and Courtship

Only a few more days remained before Christmas break, and I was anxious for it to come. I would be visiting friends, but mostly I was weary of my courses. My studies at what is now Multnomah Biblical Seminary had been exciting but intense.

But deep in my heart I almost didn't want the break to come. I was becoming more interested in Pat all the time, and when I learned she was going away over the holidays and had a few stops to make, I worried that one of those stops might be to see an old boyfriend.

So I let Pat know how I felt about her. It wasn't anything dramatic or romantic—just my usual, straight-out Latin style. I wanted her to know that she was special to me, that I cared about her a great deal, and that I hoped we could spend a lot more time together after the holidays.

I really missed her over Christmas and was anxious to get back to school. The second term was exciting, although my grades dropped a bit. Pat can take some of the credit for that, because I spent all the time with her I could!

Two words characterized our relationship during this period of courtship. One is *knowledge*. As Pat and I conversed and spent time together, I became an expert on her. I started to discover not only what she thought, but also why she felt the way she did. It's true you can love someone only to the degree you know him or her.

"Falling in love" with someone the first time you meet him or her may sound romantic, but a true love relationship won't last long on first impressions. Be careful you don't develop an idealistic image of the other person based on those impressions, because you'll be disappointed sooner or later. Honesty and openness are vital right from the start. Grow in love as you deepen in your understanding and appreciation for the other person.

The other word I want to emphasize is *spirituality*. Pat's personality, intelligence, and attractive appearance certainly caught my eye when I first met her. As we grew to know each other better, however, I discovered her deep commitment to Christ and desire to follow His will. To my mind, that was so important. At last I knew I wanted to spend the rest of my life serving the Lord together with Pat.

By the Valentine's Day banquet that year, we were unofficially engaged. I didn't exactly ask her to marry me though.

In my typical romantic fashion, as we walked under an umbrella in the Portland rain, I asked her if she would return to Latin America with me to serve the Lord there. She knew what that entailed. And I knew what her "yes" meant, too. We were married several months later.

As God's servants, we should not marry someone who is simply a Christian (1 Corinthians 7:39), but someone who is a *growing* Christian, someone whose life is marked by spirituality.

Ask yourself these questions: "Does the person I love challenge me to grow closer to the Lord? Or do I find that he or she sometimes hinders my spiritual growth?"

Decide before God to date and marry only someone with whom you could serve the Lord for a lifetime. Nothing could be more exciting or thrilling!

TO PONDER

• Why is it so easy to have an idealistic mental image of someone you love? Does such an image increase your love for that person? Why or why not?

TO PURSUE

• If you're single, go back over your list of standards for dating, courtship, and marriage, noting any changes you want to make. Develop an accountability relationship with someone in your church, making a covenant to keep those standards in obedience to the Lord.

• If you have children who aren't married yet, go back over the list of standards you want them to follow for dating, courtship, and marriage. Develop a plan to help them personalize their own list of biblical standards.

When Two
Become One

Some marriages may be made in heaven, but most of the details have to be worked out here on earth. Unfortunately, many couples enter marriage with little or no thought about how such a relationship is designed to work.

"I only married to get away from home, to get a house of my own and be independent," admitted a young woman named Jane. "My parents tried to talk me out of it, but you always think you know better."

Jane thought she was breaking from her parents. In reality, her marriage was only a contest to prove she knew best. She failed to develop a close bond with her husband, however, and "after six months I knew it was a mistake—even before my baby was born." Shortly afterward her marriage dissolved.

The names change, the circumstances vary, but the tragedy remains the same: Far too many marriages eventually end in divorce. A well-known Christian leader made this observation: "All of my counseling in marriage and family problems can be categorized on the basis of three situations: failure to truly leave the parents, failure to cleave to the one partner, or failure to develop a unified relationship."

Leave. Cleave. Unify. Moses, the Lord Jesus Christ, and later the apostle Paul all used these same three concepts to describe how God designed marriage to work. "For this reason a man will leave his father and mother and be united to his wife, and the two will become one flesh" (Mark 10:7–8).

Marriage involves leaving one's parents and clinging to our spouse. It is a total, intimate, exclusive union between a husband and his wife. But that's not all!

Christian marriage is really a triangle: a man, a woman, and Christ. My wife, Pat, committed her life to Christ at the age of eight. I was twelve when I made the same decision. When we joined our lives together, we did so in the presence of the Lord. He is the third party in our marriage. He is the One who keeps us together and draws us closer to each other as we seek to draw closer to Him.

God has designed man and woman to complement each other in the marital relationship—spiritually, intellectually, emotionally, volitionally, socially, and physically. Intimacy starts with spiritual oneness in Christ and eventually knits a couple together in every area of life. This takes time and commitment. But the rewards of such intimacy and oneness are fantastic!

"But, Luis," you say, "my spouse and I aren't experiencing that oneness in our marriage. In fact, sometimes I feel we don't even know each other. Often we disagree with each other or just go our separate ways. We're definitely not serving the Lord together. What should we do?"

When marital problems surface, don't run away from God. Instead, as God's servant, run *to* Him. Come to Christ. Lay the problem at His feet with your spouse.

Gather your spouse in your arms by your bedside. Open up your Bible, kneel together, read a passage, and talk about what it says. See what God's Word has to say about your situation. Then share your prayer requests and, together, talk to God about them. By doing this you will learn more about your spouse, and God will show you how two can become one—and grow yet closer every day.

TO PONDER

• What are some of the underlying reasons for marital conflict and divorce?

• From Mark 10:7–8, what does it mean for a man and woman to leave? cleave? unify?

TO PURSUE

• If you are married, take some time alone with your spouse to ask, "How intimate would you say we are spiritually? intellectually? emotionally? volitionally? socially? physically?"

• Also ask, "What are some practical ways you think we could begin to cultivate deeper intimacy in our marriage?"

God's Blueprint for
Happy Homes

No nation is stronger than its homes. One Chinese proverb says, "If there is harmony in the home, there will be order in the nation." The family unit is the basic foundation on which human society is built. The fragmentation of our families, however, will prove to be the destruction of our civilization.

Four prevalent attitudes attack our homes from every side. *Secularism* advocates, "Grab for all the gusto you can because you only go around once in life!" *Materialism* says, "Get more, buy more, build more!" *Sensualism* joins in by bombarding us with immorality and perversion through the media. Secular *humanism* concludes, "Glory to *man* in the highest—away with deity."

No matter what these philosophies claim, they have managed only to erode the family unit. Why? Because they oppose God's blueprint for happy homes. After all, He invented the family. And He has given us His blueprint in the Bible so we can discover what He says to spouses, parents, and children.

First of all, the Bible teaches that we are to rest in each other's strength. Ephesians 5:21 says, "Submit to one another out of reverence for Christ." Because Christ is the Lord of our family, we should treat each other with respect as He has instructed. I can't have my way all the time, nor can my wife or children. We must seek to do things God's way.

Submission is necessary for order and stability. Otherwise, everyone tries to do his or her own thing without any accountability. One hit song boasts, "I did it my way!" Go ahead and do it your way—and see how many people you hurt in the process, including yourself.

Sometimes we have this idea that the man can't show any weaknesses. He must wear a mask to cover up his true feelings. But that's false! The Bible teaches that the husband is to rely on his wife and she is to rest in him as the spiritual leader of their home.

This doesn't mean that either is inferior. Men and women are equal in God's eyes. Paul makes this clear when he says, "There is neither . . . male nor female, for you are all one in Christ Jesus" (Galatians 3:28).

God knows the family functions best with a leader. That's why He has designated the man to take that responsibility within the home and exercise it with love. Sometimes my wife, Pat, is better at making rational decisions than I am. Yet she rests upon me to make the final choices that must be made in our home. But in turn, I often rely on her counsel and advice. We complement and support each other.

As children see their parents' mutual submission to each other, they more easily respect and obey their father and mother (Ephesians 6:1–3), especially if they are disciplined in love for their own good (Hebrews 12:5–11).

God's blueprint for happy homes *does* make a difference! I encourage you to read the Bible and pray as a family each day to learn more about His blueprint for your home.

TO PONDER

• What is God's blueprint for happiness in your home? To what degree have you followed and benefited from that blueprint?

TO PURSUE

• Make a commitment to read at least one biblically based book about the family each year. I could recommend dozens of such books. Two of the best are the classic paperback *Heaven Help the Home!* by Howard G. Hendricks and the comprehensive handbook *Husbands and Wives* edited by Howard and Jeanne Hendricks (both published by Victor Books).

PART FOUR

Pursuing Victory as God's Ambassador

For the remainder of your walk, the Lord wants you to be an ambassador for Him in your home, your church, and your world.

Practicing
Family Worship

Some of the most important things you and I will ever say and do, as God's ambassadors, will be at home. That's where life's most crucial curriculum is taught to our children. On the average, our children spend one percent of their time in the church, sixteen percent in school, and the remaining eighty-three percent in and around the home.

The influence of a godly parent cannot be overestimated. Unless our children see the difference Christ makes in our lives and hear the gospel clearly presented, they will almost invariably reject Christianity.

God has no grandchildren. I discovered that as a boy. My parents both loved and served the Lord Jesus Christ. They were wonderful ambassadors for Christ. But the day came when I had to decide to commit my life to Him too.

God has designed the home as the place where His Word is to be taught, lived, and passed on from generation to generation. Deuteronomy 6:6–7 says, "These commandments that I give you today are to be upon your hearts. Impress them on your children. Talk about them when you sit at home and when you walk along the road, when you lie down and when you get up."

Someone has said, "Train up a child in the way he should go, and walk there every once in a while yourself." As our children rub shoulders with us around the table and during other times in the day, they are noticing every attitude we convey and every word we say—and carefully imitating us. Can you honestly say to your children, without embarrassment, "Follow my example, as I follow the example of Christ"? (1 Corinthians 11:1).

One of the most important ways parents communicate their faith to their children is to lead them in family worship. Time for Bible study and prayer should be a natural, enjoyable, and daily part of your family life. Involve your children in reading a short passage of Scripture and discussing what it means. Seek to be creative; it's a tragedy to bore someone when you're teaching the Bible.

Prayer is another important aspect of family worship that should extend to every part of the day—before school, during meals, and at bedtime. Teach your children to thank God for His protection and goodness, to confess their sins, and to pray for relatives and friends.

We have a stewardship with every child God gives us. Usually we have them in our home for only a comparatively short time before they leave and establish their own families. We need to pray that God will "teach us to number our days aright" (Psalm 90:12).

"Life is a short fevered rehearsal for a concert we cannot stay to give," A.W. Tozer wrote. Because our time is so limited, we must decide what we will and will not do to best bring up our children in "the training and instruction of the Lord" (Ephesians 6:4).

Make it a priority to say and do those things that will teach your children life's most important lessons. Use family worship as a means to integrate Christianity into every aspect of your home.

TO PONDER

- How was your home life growing up?
- What impact can your home make, for good, in your family? in your neighborhood? in your community? in your church?

TO PURSUE

- If you have children, do you want them to grow up with a deep-rooted love for the Lord, commitment to the church, and concern for others? If so, I recommend reading *Keeping Your Kids Christian*, edited by Marshall Shelley (Vine Books).

Understanding Who
Needs the Church

"I don't go to any church or religious meetings now," one woman acknowledged. "My religion is being with God. I don't need any help with that."

A college student added, "The church is beyond hypocrisy for me. I see it as dull, irrelevant, afraid of life, betraying God, and trying to save its own skin. There are some great individual people inside it, but they represent about one-half of one percent of the total membership. So the church for me is dead. God is very much alive, but God doesn't need the church."

Who needs the church, anyway?

A BBC journalist once asked me why I was wasting my time trying to revive and mobilize the church. Referring to Britain as a post-Christian society, he asked, "Aren't you just flogging a dead horse?"

I replied, "There is no such thing as a post-Christian society. One generation may reject the gospel itself, but it cannot reject it for future generations. And furthermore," I gladly added, "Jesus Christ specializes in raising the dead."

Who needs the church today?

I believe that we all need the church. We need to meet together as groups of believers to devote ourselves to "teaching and to the fellowship, to the breaking of bread and to prayer" (Acts 2:42).

The church, after all, is not a building or a denomination; it is *people*. And I believe that God is moving today among many Christians throughout our nation.

Are you already a member of a local church? Pray that God will move in a mighty way to revive the churches in this land.

If you have become discouraged with the church, remember what the Scripture says: "Let us not give up meeting together, as some are in the habit of doing, but let us encourage one another—and all the more as you see the Day approaching" (Hebrews 10:25).

Seek to fellowship with a church that preaches—and practices— God's Word. Too many pastors today are trying to feed their congregations social pabulum instead of truth. No wonder people are leaving the church dissatisfied!

The Lord wants to pour out His blessings in a marvelous and superlative way. And He's going to do it, I believe, as each member of the body of Christ wakes up to his or her responsibilities as an ambassador who has been called to minister within the church and to evangelize those who still need to hear the voice of God. Won't you join me in praying and working toward that end?

TO PONDER

• Do you belong to a local church? How involved are you in the life and service of your church?

• Why is active participation in a local church prerequisite for you to become one of God's ambassadors to the world?

TO PURSUE

• If you haven't already done so, take the necessary steps to become a member of your local church. Follow the Lord in baptism and regularly partake of the Lord's Supper. Practice hospitality.

• In addition, contact your pastor and volunteer to serve in some capacity. Give regularly and generously. Support your church's missionaries.

HABIT 42

Recognizing How
Any Old Bush Will Do

I've heard it said, "Whether these are the best of times or the worst of times, it's the only time we've got."

That is a good reminder for us, as God's ambassadors. This is our moment in history. We must serve the Lord daily during the time we have now. But how can we serve? How can we be victorious for Christ during our lifetime? What characterizes a genuine and successful ambassador for Christ?

Many Christians believe that if they work hard enough and pray long enough, then they'll be successful. That's the essence of legalism. As sincere as a legalist may be, if he is relying on himself, then he is heading for a terrible fall.

This was the case with Moses when he killed the Egyptian who had been beating a Hebrew slave. He was sincere in his intentions, but he was relying on his own power, the weapons of the flesh.

And this was my situation when I came to the United States in 1960 to further my biblical studies. I had big dreams I wanted to see quickly accomplished. My impatience led me to rely on my own power, not on the Lord's.

During one of the last chapel services before Christmas break, our speaker was Major Ian Thomas, founder of the Torchbearers in England. Major Thomas's theme was "Any Old Bush Will Do, As Long As God Is in the Bush."

He pointed out that it took Moses forty years in the wilderness to realize he was nothing. God was trying to tell Moses, "I don't need a pretty bush or an educated bush or an eloquent bush. If I am going to use you, *I* am going to use you. It will not be you doing something for Me, but Me doing something through you."

Major Thomas suggested that the bush in the desert was likely a dry bunch of sticks that had hardly developed, yet Moses had to take off his shoes. Why? Because this was holy ground. Why? Because God was in the bush!

I was like that bush. I could do nothing for God. All my reading, studying, asking questions, and trying to model myself after other people was worthless. Everything in my ministry was worthless unless God was in me! No wonder I felt so frustrated: Only *He* could make something happen.

When Major Thomas closed with Galatians 2:20, it all came together: "I have been crucified with Christ and I no longer live, but Christ lives in me. The life I live in the body, I live by faith in the Son of God, who loved me and gave himself for me."

I realized the secret to being a successful ambassador for Christ was depending on the indwelling, resurrected, almighty Lord Jesus Christ, and not on myself. God was finally in control of this bush!

I had tremendous peace because I realized I didn't have to struggle anymore. How sad that I had wasted eight years of my life trying to do everything in my own power.

Perhaps that is your situation today. Remember, we cannot work or earn our victories through self-effort, any more than we can work for our salvation.

Our inner resource is God Himself, because of our union with Jesus Christ (Colossians 2:9–15). Out of this understanding comes a godly sense of self-worth. I'm God's child! His pilgrim! His servant! His ambassador!

Although our days on earth are short, they can be the best of times for us. They can count for eternity if we will only come to the end of ourselves and say, "Not I, but Christ living in me."

TO PONDER

• Do you feel like an ambassador for Christ? Why or why not?

• What would have to happen for you to see yourself as God's ambassador? What would you have to do? What would God have to do? What has God already done?

TO PURSUE

• Read Exodus 3:1–4:17, the account of God's appearing to Moses in the burning bush. Underline or highlight the excuses Moses gave why he couldn't be God's ambassador. In a different color, mark God's reply to each excuse.

- In prayer, tell God you are willing to be His ambassador.

Speaking Well of
God's Son

One cold, windy night two Christian youths headed toward the tavern district in their hometown of Glasgow, Scotland, with the "preposterous" idea of holding an open-air gospel meeting. The two young men began singing hymns to gather a crowd. Their singing was tolerated, but whenever they stopped singing to share the saving message of Jesus Christ, they were mocked by the crowd with vulgar hoots and jeering howls.

Frederick S. Arnot and his friend were quite sincere about sharing their faith and the gospel message with the drunks along tavern row. Yet the crowd was determined not to let them talk. Finally, Arnot, with tears running down his face, acknowledged defeat. He and his friend turned to leave.

Suddenly someone grabbed Arnot's shoulder. Startled, Arnot turned to find a tall, elderly man towering over him. The stranger smiled warmly and said quietly, "Keep at it, laddie; God loves to hear men speak well of His Son."

With that encouragement, the two Scottish lads squared their shoulders and returned. It wasn't long before the rowdy crowd began to pay attention to the message the young men wanted to share.

In 1881, several years after this incident, Arnot, influenced by the example set by David Livingstone, left his Scottish mission field and headed for Central Africa, where God used him in a great way to proclaim the gospel.

God loves to hear men and women speak well of His Son. Yet how easy it is for us to become silent, ineffective ambassadors for Christ because of discouragement, lack of results, or some other excuse. Do you speak well of God's Son? If not, what is your excuse?

In an honest and challenging article entitled "Excuses," seminary professor Norman L. Geisler admits that even though he was in full-time Christian ministry for eighteen years, he never witnessed for Christ. His excuses sound familiar, don't they?

1. "I didn't have the gift of evangelism. It was obvious to me that someone like Billy Graham did, and it was equally obvious that I didn't."

2. "I had the gift of teaching [Christians], and it's pretty hard to make converts from that group."

3. "I didn't like . . . impersonal evangelism, so I would do 'friendship evangelism.' I wasn't going to cram the gospel down anybody's throat."

4. "I came to the conclusion that if God is sovereign . . . then He can do it with or without me."

One day, however, a visiting speaker literally demolished Geisler's excuses by saying, "I've been a missionary for years and I was never *called* . . . I was just *commanded* like the rest of you." That statement startled Geisler, and he became a fisher of men.

"Go into all the world and preach the good news to all creation" (Mark 16:15) wasn't a suggestion, but a command of the Lord Jesus Christ. Perhaps you were once eager like Arnot to witness for Christ, but somehow that zeal has faded. Remember, God loves to hear you speak well of His Son.

TO PONDER

• God has commanded you to be one of His ambassadors. How have you responded?

• When have you tried to speak well of God's Son? What happened? How did you feel afterward? Has anyone ever encouraged you to "Keep at it, laddie"?

TO PURSUE

• Review the four excuses some give for not witnessing for Christ. If you haven't spoken to anyone about Jesus Christ recently, list your excuses. Then proceed to Habit 44.

Experiencing the
Greatest Thrill

As a young man I was excited about preaching the gospel of Jesus Christ at street meetings, children's meetings, and rallies. I prayed and studied and preached, but felt frustrated.

The day came when I finally decided I didn't have the gift of evangelism, after all. It was obvious. No matter how zealously I preached, no one was coming to Jesus Christ. Nothing I did seemed to make a difference. I was inspired by the things I read and heard about Billy Graham's ministry, but I knew I didn't have what he had.

I gave God a deadline: *"If I don't see any converts through my preaching by the end of the year, I'm quitting."* Oh, I would still be an active Christian, but I would dedicate myself to teaching believers rather than evangelizing the lost.

The end of the year came and went. No converts. My mind was made up: I was through preaching. Now I was sure I didn't have the gift.

On Saturday morning about four days into the new year, the small church I attended held a home Bible study. I didn't feel like going, but I went anyway out of loyalty to the elders.

The fellow who was supposed to teach the Bible never showed up. So the man of the house said, "Luis, you are going to have to say something." I was completely unprepared.

However, I had been reading a book by Dr. Graham called *The Secret of Happiness*, which is based on the Beatitudes. So I asked for a New Testament and read Matthew 5:1–12. Then I repeated whatever I remembered from Dr. Graham's book.

As I was commenting on the beatitude "Blessed are the pure in heart, for they will see God," a lady suddenly stood up. She began to cry and said, "My heart is not pure. How can I see God? Somebody tell me how I can get a pure heart." How delightful it was to lead her to Jesus Christ!

I don't remember the woman's name, but I will never forget her words: "Somebody tell me how I can get a pure heart." Together we read in the Bible, "The blood of Jesus, his Son, purifies us from all sin" (1 John 1:7). This woman found peace with God and went home with a pure heart overflowing with joy.

When you win people to Jesus Christ, it's the greatest joy. Your graduation is exciting, your wedding day is exciting, and your first baby is exciting, but the most thrilling thing you can ever do is win someone to Christ. And it's contagious. Once you do it, you don't want to stop.

I challenge you to pray, "Dear God, I want that experience. I want to know what it is to serve as your ambassador and win someone to Jesus Christ."

Whatever our place in the body of Christ, let's enlarge our vision to invite one more person into God's kingdom. After all, God doesn't have a Plan A, a Plan B, and a Plan C for evangelizing the world. He has only one plan—and that's you and me.

TO PONDER

• In John 1, we read about Andrew, who met Jesus and then started introducing others to the Lord. Why was he so excited about telling his brother and friends about Jesus?

• Who do you know in your family, neighborhood, school, work place, and community who haven't trusted Jesus Christ yet?

TO PURSUE

• On a 3"x5" card, list the names of at least five people you know who haven't trusted Christ yet. Make a commitment to pray regularly for their salvation.

• Put a star by the name of the person you think is least likely ever to come to Christ. Pray daily for him or her. Don't be surprised if someday he or she becomes a Christian!

Catching a Vision
for Evangelism

At the end of World War II, Robert Woodruff declared, "In my generation it is my desire that everyone in the world have a taste of Coca Cola." Talk about vision!

Today Coca Cola® is sold from the deserts of Africa to the interior of China. Why? Because Woodruff motivated his colleagues to reach their generation around the world for Coke®.

How big is your vision? Have you ever dreamed about what God could do through you to help win the world in our generation to Jesus Christ? After all, as Oswald Smith said, the only generation that can reach this generation is our generation.

Even though the Lord limited His own public ministry to the Palestine area, He came and lived and died for the whole world. After His resurrection He commissioned His disciples to "make disciples of *all* nations" (Matthew 28:19, italics added). He sent them as His ambassadors first to Jerusalem, then to all Judea and Samaria, and ultimately to the ends of the earth (Acts 1:8).

Those first-century Christians were hesitant to dream about how God would fulfill Christ's last commands. The apostle Paul challenged their complacency by devoting his life after his conversion to traveling and proclaiming Christ.

Paul explained his vision for evangelism in Romans 15. First, he could report, "From Jerusalem all the way around to Illyricum, I have fully proclaimed the gospel of Christ" (Romans 15:19). Even his enemies admitted that Paul had saturated entire provinces with the gospel (Acts 19:26) and had turned the world upside down (Acts 17:6).

Paul was not content to saturate one small area with the gospel at the expense of the rest of the world. He had a strategy for reaching the entire Roman Empire. "But now that there is no more place for me to work in these regions [Jerusalem to Illyricum], and since I have been longing for many years to see you, I plan to do so when I go to Spain" (Romans 15:23–24).

Paul went on to explain his itinerary. In his mind he visualized every major city he would stop at on his way to Rome. He longed to win the people of this influential capital city to Christ—just as I long to see key cities around the world hear the voice of God. But beyond Rome, Paul ultimately wanted to reach the entire known world with the gospel of Jesus Christ.

Like Paul, as God's ambassadors our vision should be "to win as many people as possible to Jesus Christ throughout the world." That is part of my evangelistic association's statement of vision and reason for existence. Following the example of Paul, we actively and aggressively seek to evangelize the masses from city to city using every means possible.

Evangelism is not an option in the Christian life. Paul admitted, "When I preach the gospel, I cannot boast, for I am compelled to preach. Woe to me if I do not preach the gospel!" (1 Corinthians 9:16). Whether by preaching or praying, traveling around the globe or speaking to those next door, we should all have a part in winning the world to Jesus Christ.

TO PONDER

• What part can you have, through your prayers, in God's work around the world?

• How else can you be involved in helping win the world to Jesus Christ?

TO PURSUE

• Use *Operation World* by Patrick Johnstone (Zondervan) as a daily guide to pray around the world.

• Ask God to help you begin dreaming how you can be more involved in "making disciples of all nations."

Lighting the
Fires of Revival

The apostle Paul's desire to win the world to Jesus Christ always challenges me. Despite the stonings, beatings, and other hardships he endured, he sought to fan the fires of revival still brighter.

Paul used strategic thinking to carry out his ministry as an ambassador of Christ. His missionary journeys were carefully planned to saturate major cities and provinces with the gospel of Jesus Christ. He never considered it carnal or beneath his dignity to make such plans.

Even though Paul had a definite strategy to win his generation to Christ, he wasn't bound to it. He remained sensitive to the Spirit's leading. You remember how the Spirit compelled him to go to Macedonia, for instance, even though he had other plans (Acts 16).

This is an exciting concept to me. On the one hand, God intends for us to use logical, strategic planning in fulfilling the Great Commission. On the other hand, if we are sensitive to the prompting of the Spirit, God can redirect our plans when necessary. One doesn't cancel out the need for the other.

Like Paul, we need to think strategically if the whole world is to hear the voice of God. We must work and pray not only for the salvation of specific individuals, but also for the masses in large cities and nations. What would it take for them to hear and believe God's voice?

After studying the lives of Paul and other great evangelists in church history, I am convinced that God is using evangelistic crusades to touch millions of lives and bring hundreds of thousands into the kingdom of God. I am equally convinced that God uses other methods as well.

To say one form of evangelism in God's eyes is superior to another form is a serious theological flaw being heralded by some critics. Paul said, "I have become all things to all men so that by all possible means I might save some" (1 Corinthians 9:22). Witnessing to a friend is no better or worse than preaching to a multitude. God does the work, no matter what method we use. It is through the power of the Holy Spirit and by God's grace that people are saved.

The Scriptures repeatedly testify that God moves both individuals and multitudes of individuals, often after the church experiences a fresh touch of God's hand. Church history confirms this, too. But why do we always have to read about past revivals? Why can't we *live* revival in our own flesh and blood?

As Evan Roberts, the "silent evangelist" of the great Welsh revival, reminded each audience to whom he spoke, God will pour out the fires of revival only when four things happen:

1. public confession of Jesus Christ as Savior,
2. confession of every known sin,
3. the forsaking of every doubtful activity, and
4. prompt, complete obedience to the Spirit.

If these four things take place in lives throughout this land, the fires of revival could spread around the world. But what must happen before revival starts—with you?

TO PONDER

• Which do you prefer—to have a well thought out plan of action or to be more spontaneous?

• Which style (or method) of evangelism does God prefer?

TO PURSUE

• Review the four prerequisites for revival listed above. Ask God to bring revival to your own heart.

HABIT 47

Dreaming Great Dreams

When I was about seventeen years old and beginning to take the Word of God seriously, one verse bothered me. I just couldn't believe that it meant what it said. I checked other translations to see if I could find a better rendering. But the verse says essentially the same thing in each translation.

Jesus Christ declares in that verse, "I tell you the truth, anyone who has faith in me will do what I have been doing" (John 14:12).

That is a fantastic, almost incredible promise, but there it is. It came from the lips of the Lord Jesus and has been proven many times. Have you proven it true in your own life?

As a teenager growing up in Argentina, I felt frustrated about evangelizing the unsaved. "Lord, there are millions of people in this country alone," I realized. "Yet here we sit, Sunday after Sunday, the same people doing the same thing. We have to reach out."

So several of us began to pray together, "Lord, get us out of here. Do something. Use us." Slowly, in my heart and in the hearts of the others, a vision began to grow—a vision of reaching millions of people.

Some of my dreams were so wild that I didn't tell anyone except my mother about them, and I didn't even tell her all of them. She encouraged us, saying, "Come on. You don't need a special message from the Lord. He gave the order centuries ago to preach the good news to everyone. So go. Don't keep waiting for more instructions."

So we began to evangelize—slowly, in a small way. Now I am constantly amazed how the Lord has fulfilled so many of our great dreams the past thirty years. "Praise the Lord!" we've said again and again. "It's happening!"

While Jesus Christ was here among us, He deliberately limited Himself to three years of ministry in Palestine—to a small area for a short time—before dying and rising from the dead to save us.

Today Christ is calling you and me, His ambassadors, to dream great dreams because anyone who believes in Him can do the great works He did. How is that possible? The key to this promise is two-fold.

First, because Christ was going to the Father, He would send the Holy Spirit to indwell us. Now that the Spirit indwells us as believers, Christ does His works *through us!*

Second, Christ adds a condition to His promise: "Anyone who has *faith in me* will do what I have been doing" (italics added). The Lord challenges us to have faith—not necessarily to have *more* faith, but faith *in Him*. It is an ongoing faith. Another translation puts it this way: "He who continues to believe in me will also do the works that I do."

Have you stopped seeing great things happen in your life? Perhaps you have stopped believing that God can work in a mighty way even in our generation.

What limits the work of God here on earth? Is God somehow incapable of reviving the churches? Of turning the hearts of multiplied thousands to Himself? Of causing the fires of revival to spread throughout this country and beyond? Of course not!

In a sense, though, God has chosen to limit His works to those things we trust Him to do through us.

TO PONDER

- What do you wish you could do for God?
- Based on your study of God's Word, what do you believe God wants to do through you?

TO PURSUE

- Read John 14:12–15. The Lord wants us to dream great dreams. Mentally list what else He wants us to do, then proceed to Habit 48.

Planning Great Plans

We meet bored people all the time—even bored Christians. They may seem busy, but their days are filled with life's routine, ordinary chores.

As new Christians, we are thrilled by the promises of God. We get excited about answers to prayer. The biographies and books of great men and women of God challenge us to act on our faith.

But as time goes by, sometimes we become hard and cynical. We lose the joy of the Christian life and become bored. We hear of something wonderful God is doing and say "Oh," as if it's nothing!

The Lord Jesus Christ challenges us to abandon our complacency when He says, "I tell you the truth, anyone who has faith in me will do what I have been doing. He will do even greater things than these, because I am going to the Father" (John 14:12).

The Lord doesn't intend for us to sit idle and simply dream of what could happen for His glory. He wants us to plan great plans so those dreams will come true!

Someone has well said, "We believe the Lord can do anything, but we expect Him to do nothing." Often, several years after a person commits his or her life to Jesus Christ, he or she doubts God instead of continuing to trust Him for bigger things. One makes no plans bigger than oneself.

In order for God to use us again, we need to confess this unbelief and say, "Lord Jesus, renew my vision of Your power. Renew my confidence of Your abilities. Renew my trust of Your resources." Then dream and plan again.

William Carey encountered boredom and doubt when he proposed sending missionaries to evangelize around the world. Older Christians told him to give up his preposterous ideas. But in explaining his dreams and plans, Carey wrote, "Expect great things from God, attempt great things for God." That statement became the creed of the modern missions movement as men and women followed Carey's example and went to the ends of the earth with the saving message of Christ's gospel.

God burdened my own heart to win as many people as possible to Jesus Christ—first in my own city, then in my country, then in all of Latin America. Now, by God's grace, we are seeking to let the whole world hear the voice of God.

With that dream, our evangelistic association has made plans to reach the masses using the media and large evangelistic crusades in key cities. And by God's grace we are seeing some of our dreams coming true!

What about you? Are you expecting great things from God? Or are you sitting around? If it's true that the Lord Jesus Christ wants us to be His ambassadors to the nations, then we can't remain passive.

Do some dreaming. Envision the 3.5 billion people who have not heard the gospel in this generation. How could God use you to share Christ at work, at school, in your neighborhood—and beyond? Make specific plans of action. Attempt great things for God today!

TO PONDER

• What do you believe God could do in and through your life? What are you expecting Him to do?

• In what ways did the apostles fulfill Jesus' words, "[You] will do even greater things than these, because I am going to the Father"?

TO PURSUE

• Can God use you to lead someone to faith in Jesus Christ? Yes, He can! Explore what opportunities of service are available through your local church.

• Make plans now to volunteer to serve the Lord as a camp counselor, Vacation Bible School music leader, Sunday school teacher, youth group sponsor, or evangelistic home Bible study host/hostess.

Praying Great Prayers

I have a wealthy friend in Latin America who loves the Lord and loves television evangelism. On several occasions he's told me, "Luis, any time you have an evangelistic crusade, I'll pay for one night of television. If I can, I'll pay for two or three nights."

It's nice to have a friend like that! He's a marvelous person. But to be frank with you, I have the hardest time calling him. He's even told me to reverse the charges. Every once in a while he calls me. "Hey, don't you have any crusades going? You haven't called me. Don't you need any money?"

Well, of course we have crusades going, and of course we need money to proclaim the gospel. But for some reason I'm very hesitant to call him.

We're like that with the Lord. He doesn't simply challenge us to dream great dreams and plan great plans; He adds, "I will do whatever you ask in my name, so that the Son may bring glory to the Father. You may ask me for anything in my name, and I will do it" (John 14:13–14).

What an incredible promise! God wants us to ask Him for anything. Yet, even though He has called us to be His ambassadors, we hem and haw and beat around the bush. "Ask me," the Lord says. "What are you waiting for?"

When my youngest son was only six, he had a million requests. He asked me for some of the craziest things. Yet I loved to have him come and ask me. Some of his requests were too much, of course, but I didn't mind. Generally, if I could afford what he wanted, I gave it to him. He's my son.

Our heavenly Father also wants us to come to Him with our requests. He delights to give good gifts to those who ask Him (Matthew 7:11).

Notice again what the Lord stresses in John 14:13–14: "Ask in my name . . . that the Son may bring glory to the Father." He challenges us to draw on His infinite resources by asking Him in His name for anything that would glorify God. Isn't that our ultimate goal in life, anyway?

"I will do whatever you ask." I have claimed that promise many times during my life. One of my first requests was for a coin so I could get a bus ride to work in Argentina. God didn't miraculously drop the coin out of heaven, but He did supply a ride to work in an unusual way.

God has continued to answer many prayers—prayers for big decisions, desperate needs, open doors, safety, personnel, wisdom. Answers to these prayers, whether big or small, have caused my faith to grow and grow.

"Prayer is not conquering God's reluctance, but taking hold of God's willingness," Phillips Brooks said. God already knows our dreams and plans. He doesn't say, "Sell Me, convince Me!" He simply says, "Ask."

TO PONDER

• When you pray, do you ever hesitate to ask the Lord for something? Why?

• What is one of the greatest things God might be willing to do for you? Have you asked Him to do it yet?

TO PURSUE

• Take a few minutes to talk with the Lord, telling Him what's on your heart right now. Ask Him to work in and through you for His glory.

Obeying Great Commands

The sign on the stage proclaimed, "The Motionless Man: Make Him Laugh, Win $100." The temptation was irresistible. For three hours boys and girls, men and women performed every antic and told every joke they could dream up. But Bill Fuqua, the Motionless Man, stood perfectly still.

Fuqua, *Guinness Book of World Records* champion at doing nothing, appears so motionless during his routines at shopping malls and amusement parks that he's sometimes mistaken for a mannequin.

He discovered his unique talent at the age of fourteen while standing motionless in front of a Christmas tree as a joke. A woman touched him and exclaimed, "Oh, I thought it was a real person."

Doing nothing is really impossible—even for the Motionless Man. Fuqua attributes his feigned paralysis to hyperelastic skin, an extremely low pulse rate, and intense concentration. He may not laugh at your jokes, but he readily admits that he still has to breathe and blink—occasionally.

The Motionless Man reminds me of some Christians who sit still or stand around when they should be acting, speaking, moving. Do people question whether you're a real Christian? How can we serve as Christ's ambassadors and yet remain passive at the same time?

The first step in the Christian life is confessing that Jesus is Lord (Romans 10:9). As we mature, we understand more fully who Jesus really is—the King of kings and Lord of lords (1 Timothy 6:15). We discover the day is coming when every tongue shall confess that Jesus Christ is Lord (Philippians 2:11). We realize that God the Father has given Him supremacy over all creation (Colossians 1:18).

Every subsequent step in the Christian life involves obeying Jesus as Lord. The apostle John tells us, "We know that we have come to know him if we obey his commands" (1 John 2:3). To the degree that we know and believe that Jesus is Lord, to that degree we obey Him. The Bible calls this "the fear of the Lord."

The fear of the Lord implies a deep reverence and awe of God—and a corresponding response of obedience. "Blessed is the man who fears the Lord, who finds great delight in his commands" (Psalm 112:1).

The Lord Jesus calls us not only to dream great dreams, to plan great plans, and to pray great prayers, but also to obey His great commands: "If you love me, you will obey what I command" (John 14:15). The Lord's commands are always great. He never gives little, puny suggestions.

Listen to His last words before His ascension: "All authority in heaven and on earth has been given to me." He is the Lord of lords. "Therefore go and make disciples of all nations, baptizing them in the name of the Father and of the Son and of the Holy Spirit, and teaching them to obey everything I have commanded you. And surely I am with you always, to the very end of the age" (Matthew 28:18–20). As Lord, He has given us a great commission.

The Lord has not called us to sit around motionless. He's called us to action! Let's move ahead as His ambassadors and enjoy the excitement of obeying Him and inviting people to come into His kingdom.

TO PONDER

• Have you publicly confessed Jesus as Lord of your life? Do you really believe He is Lord? If so, have you been actively obeying and serving Him? Why or why not?

• What does it mean to fear the Lord? Is that something God calls you to do as His child? As His pilgrim? As His servant? Or as His ambassador?

TO PURSUE

• Right now, make a commitment before the Lord to obey (and teach) all that He commands.

Finishing the
Unfinished Task

Imagine what would happen if every man, woman, and child in your area heard the gospel of Jesus Christ proclaimed clearly and committed their lives to Him this year. Every newspaper around the world would take notice! Every radio station would report "the greatest revival of all time." Every television newscast would discuss the dramatic reformation taking place here.

But our work would *not* be finished. What about the new children? What about the future immigrants? And what about the more than 3.5 billion people who have never heard a clear presentation of the gospel?

Statistics overwhelm us. So let's think about the specific individuals we know and have met who have never committed their lives to Jesus Christ. Who comes to mind? Then think about the crowds you see in the cities—in shopping malls, along busy streets, everywhere. How do you feel when you think about them?

Scripture tells us that when Jesus saw the crowds, "He had compassion on them, because they were harassed and helpless, like sheep without a shepherd" (Matthew 9:36). We need to ask God to move our hearts with the same compassion that moves His heart.

The greatest dangers we face as Christians are cynicism and a cool detachment. "Oh, yes, so more than 3.5 billion don't know Christ. That's too bad." We must not forget the actual *people*, including those we know and love, behind that number who live "without hope and without God in the world" (Ephesians 2:12).

The Lord pointed out the urgency of our task by reminding His disciples, "The harvest is plentiful but the workers are few" (Matthew 9:37). We must sense the urgency of our time. How long must people wait before they hear the gospel? How many more generations must pass before some parts of the world hear the message of Christ for the first time?

It's exciting to see that in most of the so-called Third World today there is a tremendous harvest. Several nations in Latin America and Africa could become fifty-one percent Christian within the next decade. And God is at work in an amazing way throughout Asia, Eastern Europe, and the former Soviet republics. Mass communications have made it possible to reach even "closed" nations with the message of life.

But our task is urgent. That's why Jesus Christ commanded His disciples, "Ask the Lord of the harvest, therefore, to send out workers into his harvest field" (Matthew 9:38). Our Bibles end the chapter right there, but don't stop reading! In the next five verses the Lord gave His disciples authority and sent them out into the harvest. The Twelve became an answer to their own prayer!

In order to finish the task we must have the authority of God that comes from a holy life. Paul told Timothy, "God did not give us a spirit of timidity, but a spirit of power, of love and of self-discipline" (2 Timothy 1:7). I like to think of this as holy boldness.

The unfinished task of winning the world to Jesus Christ is enormous. As an ambassador of Christ, are you willing to gain a compassion for the unsaved and a sense of urgency in reaching them for Christ? Are you available to God to serve with holy boldness as a worker in His harvest? Let's press on to finish the task set before us.

TO PONDER

• Who do you know who is "without hope and without God in the world"? Are they happy the way they are? What difference could Christ make in their lives?

• Some eighty-five percent of those who trust Jesus Christ do so before age eighteen. What does that suggest about the importance of evangelizing children?

TO PURSUE

• Support your church's outreach to the children and youth in your community, and your local Christian camp.

• In addition, I recommend phoning 1-800-336-7676 to ask Compassion International how you can have an active part in helping win the children of the world to Jesus Christ through Compassion's excellent child sponsorship program.

Making the Most
Important Decision

As Christians we can all look back to the time in our lives when we made a commitment to Jesus Christ. I made that crucial decision while attending a two-week summer camp in the mountains of Argentina.

Charles Cohen, one of my professors at the boarding school I attended as a boy, organized the camp each summer. My tent counselor's name was Frank Chandler.

Every night of the week during summer camp, Mr. Chandler would wake up one boy, get him out of bed, and—with a Bible in one hand and a flashlight in the other—take the boy outside. There, under the stars, he would sit down with the boy and lead him to faith in Christ.

Even though I felt guilty for my sins and knew I needed to make a Christian commitment, I didn't want to face up to the issue with anyone. But eventually every other boy had talked to Mr. Chandler. When he came into the tent that last night of camp, I knew why!

I pretended I was asleep, thinking he would go away. It didn't work. "Come on, Palau," he said, "get up." I didn't know it, but this was going to be the best night of camp. We went outside and sat down on a fallen tree. "Luis," Mr. Chandler asked, "are you a Christian or not?"

I said, "I don't think so."

"Well, it's not a matter of whether you think so or not. Are you or aren't you?"

"No, I'm not."

"If you died tonight, would you go to heaven or hell?"

I sat quietly for a moment, a bit taken back, and then said, "I'm going to hell."

"Is that where you want to go?"

"No," I replied.

"Then why are you going there?"

I shrugged my shoulders. "I don't know."

Mr. Chandler then turned in his Bible to Romans and read: "If you confess with your lips, Luis, that Jesus is Lord, and believe in your heart, Luis, that God raised him from the dead, you, Luis, will be saved. For man believes with his heart and so is justified, and he confesses with his lips and so is saved" (Romans 10:9–10 RSV, adapted).

He looked back at me. "Luis, do you believe in your heart that God raised Jesus from the dead?"

"Yes, I do," I replied.

"Then what do you have to do next to be saved?"

I hesitated, so Mr. Chandler had me read Romans 10:9 once more—"If you confess with your lips, Luis, that Jesus is Lord . . . you will be saved."

Mr. Chandler put his arm around me and led me in prayer. I opened my heart to Christ right there, out in the rain, sitting on a log, in a hurry. But I made my decision. I was only twelve years old at the time, but I knew I was saved. I had eternal life because Jesus Christ said, "I give them eternal life, and they shall never perish; no one can snatch them out of my hand" (John 10:28).

I could hardly sleep, I was so excited about committing my life to Christ! After all, it is the most important decision anyone can ever make. When you think about it, compared to receiving eternal life, no other decision is nearly that important.

C.S. Lewis said it well: "No man is ready to live life on earth until he is ready for life in heaven." Together let's proclaim the gospel wherever the Lord leads so as many people as possible can be ready.

TO PONDER

- What was your life like before you came to Christ?
- How did you become a Christian?
- How has your life been different since becoming a Christian?

TO PURSUE

- Take a few minutes to outline your testimony, answering the "To Ponder" questions listed above.

• Ask God to give you an opportunity to share your testimony with a fellow Christian this week.

• Then, ask the Lord to give you boldness to share it with someone who doesn't know Christ yet.

RECOMMENDED READING

To further enrich your Christian life, look for the following books in your local Christian bookstore. If the store doesn't have one of these books in stock, ask the sales clerk to order it for you.

Heaven Help the Home! by Howard G. Hendricks (Victor Books)
Husbands and Wives edited by Howard and Jeanne Hendricks with LaVonne Neff (Victor Books)
Keeping Your Kids Christian by Marshall Shelley (Vine Books)
Measure Your Life by Wesley L. Duewel (Zondervan)
My Utmost for His Highest by Oswald Chambers (Discovery House)
The One Year Bible (Tyndale)
Operation World by Patrick Johnstone (Zondervan)
Practical Christianity edited by LaVonne Neff, et. al. (Tyndale)
Say Yes! How to Renew Your Spiritual Passion by Luis Palau (Multnomah)
The Secret of Happiness by Billy Graham (Word)
What Is a Real Christian? by Luis Palau (Multnomah)
You Can Trust the Bible by John R.W. Stott (Discovery House)

ABOUT THE AUTHOR

Who is Luis Palau? Perhaps you've followed his ministry with interest for years. Or perhaps this book is your first introduction to the man.

Luis Palau is now becoming well known in his adopted homeland, America. His popularity in Latin America, the United Kingdom, and other parts of the world is rather remarkable.

During one crusade, more than 518,000 people in London turned out to hear Luis Palau in person. And a crowd of 700,000 people gathered to hear Luis on Thanksgiving Sunday in Guatemala a few years ago.

In many ways, Luis Palau stands out in this generation as a truly international Christian spokesman and leader. He's a third generation transplanted European who grew up in the province of Buenos Aires, Argentina, and then chose to become an American citizen after completing the graduate course at Multnomah Biblical Seminary in Portland, Oregon.

Equally at ease in English and Spanish, Luis Palau's solidly biblical, practical messages hit home in the minds and hearts of listeners around the world.

"Luis is probably more in demand among evangelicals to preach and speak than almost any other person in the world," says Billy Graham. "Wherever there is an evangelical conference they try to get Luis Palau, because he is a powerful preacher. But more than that, he is an evangelist to whom God has given a multiplicity of gifts."

Luis Palau has proclaimed the Good News of Jesus Christ to hundreds of millions of people via radio and television in ninety-five countries, and face-to-face to more than eleven million people on six continents.

The impact? Many thousands of people have trusted Jesus Christ and become established as disciples in local churches. Cities and nations have heard a clear proclamation of the gospel. Luis Palau's burden is to see the same thing happen in America, in this generation.

Luis and his wife, Pat, also a popular conference speaker and author, have served as missionary-evangelists in Costa Rica, Colombia, and Mexico. The Palaus have four grown sons and now make their home in Portland, Oregon, near the international headquarters of the Luis Palau Evangelistic Association.

CORRESPONDENCE

If this book has motivated you to develop healthy habits for spiritual growth, or if you have been helped in any other way through the varied ministries of the Luis Palau Evangelistic Association, please let me know. My address is:

Luis Palau
P.O. Box 1173
Portland, OR 97207
USA